In *Leaving Aberdeen: Memoir of*
serves as a time-travel guide who
of what it was like to live in mid-twentieth century America. Hers is an
insightful bildungsroman and #ownvoices account that connects to other
Southern US Black women's nonfiction narratives such as bell hooks' *Bone
Black* and Eloise Greenfield's *The Great Migration: Journey to the North* as
well as realistic fiction like Mildred Taylor's *All the Days Past, All the Days
to Come* and Gwendolyn Brooks' *Maud Martha*. Make a cup of tea, find a
quiet spot, sit and enjoy.

~Jené Watson, librarian, educator, and author of
The Spirit That Dreams: Conversations with Women Artists of Color

Leaving Aberdeen is more than just a heartwarming memoir. Ms. Estell's
story, chronicling her rise from a Southern Mississippi girl in the 1940s
and '50s to being a bonafide woman, wife, and mother in New York City
during the 1960s to her current life as a grandmother and college graduate
in Georgia. Coupled with a multitude of major societal events occurring
within the last eight decades, this book speaks to her continued ability to
grow, embrace change, and triumph in the face of adversity. All who embark
upon this journey will undoubtedly be inspired by the life, times, and legacy
of Ms. Estell Halliburton.

~Dr. Natasha N. Johnson, faculty, Georgia State University

Leaving Aberdeen: Memoir of a Southern Girl is such a captivating chronicle
of Estell's life journey. It is filled with moving, descriptive language that
subtly transports the reader to another place and time. It is a beautiful,
riveting saga of becoming and overcoming, a true testament to the power
of love, the value of support, and the pricelessness of believing in a person.
Like a fine tapestry, Estell has woven those characters into her story and
made them alive and part of the reader's life. Reading this book, one will
travel through a plethora of emotions, as it also speaks the truth of racism
and injustice of the era.

Aberdeen does not gloss over the immense racism that "colored" people
were forced to endure in silence. The pain of such experiences test one's
resolve, but in Aberdeen, the Sims family courageously maintained their
dignity.

Beautiful, tender, touching, nostalgic, *Leaving Aberdeen: Memoir of a Southern Girl* is is a prominent exhibition of love, family, and the resilience of the human spirit.

~Angela G. Veal

Estell presents several extremely insightful personal experiences of a young black girl growing up in southern Mississippi. If you think you know the hard lives she and other blacks endured in the second half of the twentieth century, her real-life examples will open your eyes further. Estell closes by showing how anyone who has the strong desire and commitment to being unique and successful can do it.

~Rick Wemmers, business executive

Estell Halliburton is a trailblazer providing first-person testimony about her family's individual experience in the Great Migration of Blacks to the North that unfolded (for them) during the 1960s. Halliburton's debut memoir, *Leaving Aberdeen: Memoir of a Southern Girl,* will draw you in with plain talk and southern charm as only she can deliver it.

Halliburton weaves a compelling account of her journey from protected childhood in segregated Aberdeen, Mississippi to young womanhood on the threshold of an uncertain future when she arrives in New York in search of a better life. In the tradition of African philosophy, she looks back to the past in celebration of her ancestors who sacrificed for that "better life" even as she reclaims the present and future revisiting Aberdeen with a passion to cultivate racial acceptance and equality through her writing.

You will see glimpses of Black love, family togetherness, self-education, and activism that all conspired together to help them succeed through migration. I recommend this book "to share what our lives were like ... for all African Americans who share this history and for everyone else who can learn from it."

~Rev. Sherri Banks

Leaving Aberdeen

Memoir of a Southern Girl

ESTELL SIMS HALLIBURTON

ISBNs:
978-1-7374462-0-0 (paperback)
978-1-7374462-2-4 (hardcvoer)
978-1-7374462-1-7 (eBook)

Halliburton Publishing Co., LLC
PO Box 567191
Atlanta, Georgia 31156

Edited by Candace Johnson, Change It Up Editing

Cover illustration and cover design by Jennifer Pradhan

Interior design by Jera Publishing

Unless otherwise noted, all photos © Estell Sims Halliburton

Disclaimer: The author has tried to re-create events, locales, and conversations from her memories of them. Some names and identifying details have been changed to protect the privacy of individuals.

"Stand up straight and realize who you are,
that you tower over your circumstances."

~ Maya Angelou, American poet and civil rights activist

"We wear the mask that grins and lies,
it hides our cheeks, and shades our eyes."

~ Paul Laurence Dunbar, African American poet and novelist

This book serves to keep our memories alive.

I dedicate this book to my parents, Wardell Sims and Estell Sims.

My home on Matubba Street in Aberdeen, Mississippi, was as joyful as being wrapped in a warm blanket. I was a rather naughty child, which tested my parents' patience, but they never wavered in their love for me.

In addition to their struggles to hold our family together, Momma and Daddy endured daily indignities. I did not appreciate the sacrifice that they made for our family when I was growing up.

My home was a refuge of kindness and love. I am grateful that my parents provided me with a nurturing home where I felt safe. I will always cherish their memories!

⌒

In the summer of 1964, I got off the Trailways bus in New York City at the Port Authority near Forty-Second Street. My cousin from Aberdeen picked me up at the station and introduced me to Joseph R. Halliburton that first day. He had broad shoulders, walnut-brown skin, and an accent that was different from that of any guy I'd met in Aberdeen. Joseph showed me so many possibilities, and I wanted to be a part of his life.

Months later, I married this handsome soldier. Although our life together was often difficult, it was worthwhile. I will never forget his smiles at our daughters and grandchildren. I will always love you, Joseph.

Contents

Foreword

My parents raised my two sisters and me in the South. Since my older sister and I were born in New York where my father's family lived, I took the attitude of many Northerners. I believed that the South was a backward place with antiquated rituals and beliefs. That belief even impacted how I thought about my mother, who grew up during a time that few of us can remember or will ever experience. It influenced her in so many ways. Now that I am older, I understand my mother's "origin story."

Growing up, I never really knew my mother. She always took care of us and worked long hours. Her quiet demeanor made her an ever-present background player in our young lives. My father's large personality dominated our family, so I never gave much thought to my mother's past. Infrequent trips to her home town in Mississippi for visits and mostly funerals never shed much light.

Throughout my childhood, my mother's Southern heritage always stood out. She encouraged us to always have manners. I still catch myself saying, "I beg your pardon." When others were rude, we were taught to be polite, and to respect our elders. We ate fried chicken at least once a week. No meal was ever complete without sweet tea. I always imagined my mother growing up in a segregated but joyful environment filled with school, church, and family gatherings.

Maybe my mother wanted us to believe that because it was easier than the truth.

Many people believe that the civil rights movement of the 1960s began with people like Malcolm X and Martin Luther King, Jr. But the yearning for equality existed in the hearts of Black people across America. Although many felt powerless to enact change on a large scale, their lives provided a living, breathing testimony of the transformation occurring across America.

As I read the pages of my mother's story, I recognized the first of a series of transformations that continue until this day. My father's death in March of 2010 changed her in ways I could not have imagined. She began to realize her value, and this gave her a voice. In this book, my mother chronicles the story of her life growing up in a racist and segregated community in Mississippi. She gives a voice to family members who are no longer here. She provides a glimpse of what it felt like to make the journey from the South to the North to find new opportunities like so many others during the Great Migration. When reading her story, I am transported to the past in a time before Black Lives Mattered and our country's first African American president. Picking cotton and living in left over slave quarters were the norm.

I hope the reader of this book appreciates this glimpse into the past through one woman's eyes. Her story is our family's story. Our story is an American story.

Rabia Nelson
May 2021

Introduction

I came from a humble beginning. I am the daughter of Wardell and Estell Sims. I grew up in Mississippi, and my family were sharecroppers on a plantation. Even though we weren't slaves, we were still impacted by poverty and racism in the segregated South of the 1950s. This book is about my journey to a life I never could have imagined then.

After my sister's funeral in 2015, I decided that I was going back to college, just like she and I had talked about, and I would write my story about our lives on the plantation. With my family gone, I knew I had to carry the torch to tell our story. This is such a heavy burden, and it is lonely without them. But I feel it is important to share what our lives were like in as much detail as I can remember—not just for my family and our descendants, but for all the African Americans who share this history and for everyone else who can learn from it.

My goal in writing this book is to channel my hopes, fears, and emotions into a narrative so others can know what our lives were like so those who shared a similar experience can feel heard. I wrote this book because I didn't see my story on the bookshelf. And this is also a passion project to reveal facets of my character that I had concealed for years. Writing this book has stirred up many painful memories I've carried for years inside of me, and happy moments too.

My love for my family brought me so much joy, even during the time of living in poverty. Being rejected because of the color of my skin only strengthened my desire to continue my journey to be *free*. I hope to shed light on a period of history that many people believe did not exist or thought happened a long time ago.

I first thought about writing this book twenty years ago. A decade later, when I visited the Evans Memorial Library on Long Street in Aberdeen, Mississippi in 2010, the shelves were empty of books about Shivers High … but the white high school's yearbooks were there. Our Black lives in Aberdeen seemed invisible.

A portrait of my dad, Wardell Sims, wearing his overalls and a plaid shirt, had hung for years on the wall of the Aberdeen City Hall, the marble building on Commerce Street. His picture had been in the *Aberdeen Examiner* newspaper for his service to the city under four mayors. However, when I visited Aberdeen in 2018, the framed picture of my dad had disappeared; someone had ripped it from the wall, but no one at Aberdeen City Hall seemed to know what had happened to it. I thought, *What am I going to do about this?* That's when I decided to tell my story about my family.

Even though my dad had only a fourth-grade education, he was my hero. He was not an ordinary man; he possessed the courage and dignity that paved the way for my family and me. When I was a little girl, I saw my dad going to the back door of Tony Café on Commerce Street many times to eat a hamburger while the white people were eating in the front. Yet my dad held his head high, and he continued working until he was ninety years old. This gnawed at me, and I thought, *I need to tell my story. The Evans library should foster more stories about our rich history and other ethnic groups as well.*

I am writing for self-discovery and because of the importance of family. Despite this incident of trying to erase my dad's memory, I am committed to bringing awareness to our rich history. Indeed, I found new energy while writing my memoir and thinking about the injustices that I have witnessed in my journey. Yet, I have also learned many lessons as a daughter, a wife, and a mother. The fear that I felt is no longer holding me back; today, I am confident that I am ready to make my own choices.

1

My Early Life on the Plantation

I WAS BORN ON a Monday night in 1945, the youngest of four children, in a two-room wooden house with a tin roof. My momma told me I was a fine baby girl and that after my birth, my daddy used a kerosene lamp to watch over us. Our place was about five miles from Aberdeen, Mississippi. My family were sharecroppers on a small plot of land. Although I didn't know it at the time, my childhood experiences were very different from those of many children of my generation.

Our house, with a faded #5 on the mailbox, was on a gravel road. There was a brick fireplace to keep us warm but no electricity or running water. Sitting by the fireplace was fun. Although my knees got burned from the fire, it was a way to stay warm even when the cracked windows in the bedroom let in the cold winter air. The houses were far apart, but all the families pumped water from the wells located in the middle. I enjoyed hearing the women singing hymns while pumping water.

Momma prepared our food on a wood stove with a chimney that smoked up the kitchen. Daddy pumped water from a well that was a deep hole in the ground to feed the hogs. My brothers hauled water to wash our hands and to bathe. It took about three buckets of water to clean our vegetables and hog meat. My twelve-year-old sister, Mary, had to push the pump handle with both hands to pull up the water, and I often went to the well with her. At five years old, I carried water in a small tin bucket, and I was barefoot with mud between my toes. I had one pair of Sunday shoes and a pair of shoes for school.

As I grew older, I began to realize that my family was struggling to survive.

Although we did not have much in the way of possessions, we had each other. My brother Alfred was the oldest. He was tall, with broad shoulders, and he liked to go hunting with my dad for rabbits and was handy with tools. My younger brother, Wardell, was of average height, and he taught Sunday school at Mount Union Church as a teenager. He enjoyed reading *The Adventures of Tom Sawyer* in the outhouse. My brothers were best friends, and they spent hours together just roaming in the woods.

During deer season, Daddy took the boys hunting. Alfred got the weapons cleaned and ready to use. He made sure the shotguns had shells. He wore his overalls and carried a burlap sack for food. My brother enjoyed sleeping in the woods and searching for deer. Alfred took pride in leading his family on the hunt.

Alfred, tall and handsome, was my hero. He made me a small fishing rod and took me fishing at the pond on Saturday afternoons. He was always energetic and happy.

I enjoyed twisting around and throwing dishes up in the air like a ball; Alfred told Momma not to spank me when I broke her dishes. Once when I was feeding our two hogs, I opened pen's gate, and they ran into the pasture. I saw these short-legged, red-haired hogs with long snouts running wild, and I knew I was in trouble. Alfred was playing with his bow and arrow in the yard and saw what had happened, so he came running to catch the hogs. He herded them back into the pen by wrestling them to the ground. By the time he finished, his clothes were caked with mud, and he smelled like rotten meat.

Mary took pride in Alfred being her big brother because when the boys would bully her and call her Skinny Legs, Alfred had a talk with them. Other times, he came home with a bloody nose from defending his sister.

Mary, who was seven years older than me, was tall, skinny, and quiet. She received good grades from her teacher at the one-room schoolhouse in the woods. She loved her gray cat, Bubba. He was always lying in her lap on the porch. Mary had a talent for sewing and threading a needle like my momma, who made most of our clothing out of flour sacks.

Mary had long braids that hung to her shoulders. She would comb my short and matted hair for Sunday school and put lotion on my dry knees. On Saturdays, Mary pushed me high in the swing that was attached to an oak tree. I held on tightly to the rope, but sometimes I'd still fall off and scrape my knee on the ground. I'd jump back on the swing for the excitement of feeling the fresh breeze on my face.

My brother Wardell, nicknamed Junior, was the only one who would pull me in my red wagon up and down the hill when he finished his chores. He enjoyed playing baseball, and he thought he could run like Jackie Robinson. After supper, he allowed me to play with his baseball bat and gloves, which made me happy. Our two cousins, Cliff and Melvin, Uncle Roosevelt's children who lived down the road, joined the team. They liked playing ball because they did not have to think about picking cotton in the hot sun and walking behind a mule to plow up a field.

Daddy sometimes bought cloth from the Woolworth store in town, and Momma used it to sew us gingham dresses and shirts. Momma canned peaches, pickles, and collard greens from our back-yard garden. We had one cow named Buttercup, my dad allowed me to milk her with him in the barn. In the afternoon, we churned the milk and made butter in our kitchen.

I had quite a sweet tooth growing up on the plantation. And I looked forward to eating homemade peanut brittle candy made with sorghum molasses. I preferred sugar sandwiches and rice with a spoon of sugar for breakfast. When Wardell went to town, he would buy me a coconut candy bar with rainbow colors. I usually put this candy in my pocket and saved a piece for Spooky, my German shepherd with black and tan fur, who had been a gift from my dad for my fifth birthday. For my sixth birthday, Momma baked me a hummingbird cake with three layers and thick white icing. I shared it with my classmate, Betty Lou, who assisted me in blowing out my candles. Daddy bought me a pair of pink sandals and told me to throw away my old white sandals with their peeling leather. I danced around in my new shoes for hours.

Often, I had pork sausages for breakfast. For dinner, I preferred fresh corn on the cob from the field, ham hocks, mustard greens, and cast-iron skillet corn bread. Momma expected me to eat the fried hind legs of a rabbit from the woods that Daddy killed the day before. Momma always told me to finish my plate, but I did not care for rabbits or crackling bread, so I would feed that to Spooky, who lay under the table in the kitchen just waiting for his treats.

⁓

My daddy was Wardell Sims from the small town of Prairie, Mississippi. His parents were Alfred and Annie Sims, and he had six brothers and one sister. The family owned their land, and they were farmers. Daddy had only a fourth-grade education, but he knew how to calculate figures mentally, and he eventually came to own his own home in Aberdeen.

In December of 1925, my dad married my mother, Estell Pruitt, and they were married for fifty-five years until Momma passed in 1993.

My momma's mother was Mary Jane Pruitt. I don't recall Momma's father's name. Momma had three sisters, Gracie, Allie, and Sylvester. I don't know much about my ancestors, and as of this writing, I am still searching for information about my family's heritage.

Momma lived with her family on a plantation before she met my dad. Her uncles were schoolteachers, but Momma was unable to finish her schooling because she had to quit school to work in the field.

Daddy was working in a sawmill with other Colored men in Prairie, Mississippi when his friend Abraham was found floating in the river by the building with his feet bound together for asking for his paycheck. Daddy quit his job because he felt his life was in danger. Afterward, he was unable to find work to take care of us, his family. Finally, he found a place for us on the Thompson plantation as a sharecropper along with his brother, Roosevelt.

༄

Sharecropping thrived in Aberdeen, Mississippi, until 1960. It was a result of the devastated economy in the South during the Reconstruction era after the Civil War. Neither formerly wealthy landowners nor poor white farmers had any money to pay taxes or hire laborers. Most of the former slaves who stayed in the South could work but didn't own land or have money to purchase any property. Sharecropping was the solution for many, with the crops focused primarily on cotton, and the "croppers" or tenant farmers working the land and the landowners closely supervising the tenants. My dad, Wardell Sims, was a sharecropper. He was allowed to use the land in exchange for a share of the crop. After I left the plantation, I never talked about picking cotton, being barefooted, and living in a shack. Years later, when I went to college at Tuskegee Institute (now Tuskegee University) in 1964, I registered for an American history class. I was in an old wooden building with a quaint smell. My bald professor stood at his podium while he talked about slavery and Reconstruction. I scooted down in my seat and closed my eyes because the topic of America's past made me angry and sad. My entire life, the hardships brought upon my family by segregation, were never discussed, not in school and not at home. I always thought freedom was unreachable.

He lectured about how the churches played an important role in the lives of Blacks by teaching them skills to be independent and by providing them a safe place to worship. We also learned that newly freed slaves were able to vote after Reconstruction. Many former slaves were elected to Congress from the South in 1870, and at least one was appointed after serving in the Mississippi state legislature. The professor showed a poster of Black congressmen who were dressed in suits with a vest, bow ties, pocket watches, and trimmed hair styles. With hard work, these free men were able to integrate with whites and exert economic success.

I sat up in my seat. I had never heard this in Aberdeen. My teacher explained that this freedom held by Blacks did not last long because whites felt humiliated and cheated. So, the Ku Klux Klan and other white supremacy groups began to terrorize Blacks, which eroded our voting rights. Jim Crow laws and other methods were enacted to further undermine our rights. After class finished, I held my head up in pride because my folks possess courage. I saw that our people had voted before 1960 and even held power.

Moreover, there were many people like my parents who were unable to find work to raise their families. During this time, these wealthy white landowners became plantation owners. The tenants like my dad were in debt with the landowners for our home and livestock. As a sharecropping family, we were tied to the land like other tenants who were drowning in debt with no way out.

∽

My family worked the land for Mr. Thompson, a big man who chewed tobacco and wore a silver pistol on his hip. He owned the plantation of 100 acres of land, and there were five families living there and working their individual plots. We called it "The Quarters." As tenants, we could use the land in return for a share of the crop. My Uncle Roosevelt and his ten children lived there, too.

Our days began at 4:00 a.m. when the rooster crowed, and we crawled out of bed. The first thing I smelled was ground coffee brewing in the kettle on the stove. Mary rolled out the dough for biscuits on the kitchen table, and Momma cooked our breakfast of biscuits with thick gravy and a piece of lean fatback meat. Momma had breakfast ready promptly at 6:40 a.m. We quickly ate our meat and bread off a tin pan because we had a thirty-minute ride to the fields. It was a bumpy ride to the field with my brother Alfred pulling the reins on our horse, Sam.

My family owned our wagon, which often broke down on our way to the field. I'd sit on the back, chewing on dried peanuts, with my legs hanging down next to the hoes, sacks to pick the cotton, and tin buckets that held our fatback, biscuits, and sweet potatoes. Sitting beside me was my sister, Mary, who shared her bubble gum with me.

When I turned six years old, Momma made a small sack for me to pick cotton, which I dragged behind me like my sister did. During picking season, with the sizzling hot sun beaming down on our faces, we harvested enough cotton to make 500-hundred-pound bales, which daddy could sell for twenty dollars each. To pay the landowners, my family worked six days a week; Sundays were for church.

Picking cotton was back-breaking labor because we stayed bent over at the waist dragging a 60- to 100-pound sack for hours. Momma and Daddy wore beige cotton sacks across their backs till dusk. The cotton was about waist high with sharp edges, which made my momma's fingers bleed. Momma was sick with swollen legs, but she never quit picking cotton. Her back was sore from bending from morning

till the sun went down. She crawled on her knees to drag the heavy
sacks, which we all dragged behind us. Daddy and my brothers picked
about 200 pounds a day; my mom averaged 150 pounds, and my sister
picked around 100 pounds. Our fingers were scratched from burs
(the pointed edges of cotton buds), and the sacks hurt our shoulders.

Most days, I picked forty pounds of cotton. I wore my straw hat
and raggedy overalls, sometimes with high-top shoes, but most of
the time, I stepped barefooted on the red dirt. When I got tired of
standing, I crawled on my knees. My small hands were scarred, and
my fingernails were brittle from the sharp edges of the cotton buds.
Other times, I was bitten by small spiders, which caused itching and
swelling on my arms. The sun beating on my face made my skin dry,
and then it peeled from the sweltering heat. I cried many days to
go home and play with my dog, Spooky. When Momma heard me
whimpering, she would rock me in her lap and hug me. Then, I had
to continue picking cotton until sundown.

Our family worked even if we were sick because losing our home
and our right to work the land was always a risk.

One afternoon, my sister's face grew red from the sizzling hot
sun, and her nose began to bleed. Seeing a doctor wasn't an option;
all we had were home remedies. Momma rushed to pour water on
Mary's head, and her eyes were blurry. Momma placed a bunch of
keys around her neck. Putting keys around Mary's neck was a folk
remedy to cure the bleeding.. I crawled under the wagon to lay beside
my sister, and I rubbed her head for hours, crying for her to wake
up. The bleeding finally stopped, and I was so happy when her eyes
snapped open. I hugged her around the neck.

On Saturday afternoons, I found a way to sneak into the woods to
roll in the leaves with Spooky. My chores at six years old were milking
the cow and feeding the hogs with leftover bones and biscuits from our
table. That was not fun, but in the woods, I had fun seeing the rabbits
running up tree limbs and playing on the tire swing that my brother

Alfred had made for me. I liked to twirl around in my overalls and a straw hat and pick blueberries, even though I was afraid of the snakes hiding under the leaves. Yet I wanted to see if the snakes had fangs, so I'd poke at them with my stick. Alfred knew my hangout, and he would often scold me for running off. I got tired of folks telling me what to do.

⌒

My dad was fortunate that he was able to repay Mr. Thompson, the landowner. Usually, sharecroppers were there until they got too old to work or died from working like a mule. Many of these people never knew they could vote or leave the plantation for a better life. They were stuck in poverty, but they held to their belief in God and their families and that one day they would be free. I know that when I left the plantation, I finally saw my dad smiling and my momma humming in the kitchen.

Mr. Thompson came to see Daddy every month. Daddy pretended to be friendly, but he was boiling with anger because he seemed to be deeper in the hole every year. One day, Mr. Thompson came to see my dad to remind him that he needed to farm more land in exchange for his house. Daddy was six feet tall and muscular and of mixed race with a lighter skin tone.

I listened by the fence to this loud man with a mean face who wore a cowboy hat. When he spoke to my dad, it sounded like curse words, which made me sad. While Mr. Thompson talked, Daddy folded his arms, and his face was blank and stiff. When Mr. Thompson left, Daddy's lips were tight; this man provoked Daddy. He walked to the porch and opened his small Bible, trying to calm the storm inside. He turned the pages of his Bible to the Old Testament and began humming "Amazing Grace."

My legs felt weak, and I balled up my hands. I wasn't hungry for the rest of the afternoon; I just wanted to comfort my dad. Daddy did not mention Mr. Thompson, but his lips poked out when he spoke about him. I followed my dad to the porch and sat beside him with my dog, Spooky. My puppy often slept near my bed, and he was my constant companion, especially when I went to pick berries in the woods. But that day, Spooky and I sat with my dad to let him know that I loved him. Later, Daddy uttered, "That man is wicked." I knew that Mr. Thompson had dampened Daddy's spirit, but he never wavered in his will to hold onto our family and protect us.

Many times, the money came up short at the end of the year, so my dad raised white chickens with red beaks that produced pearly white eggs. Daddy had a collie, a shaggy dog, called Old Joe, who ran after the chickens in the yard even though he was about fifteen years old and missing most of his teeth. Daddy sold the eggs from a basket at a small roadside market near the plantation. He learned to fix the roof on the barn and broken wagon wheels. And he buried sweet potatoes in a mound like a pyramid, which allowed them to remain fresh to eat during the winter. In December, he gathered with the other men to kill hogs at dawn and butcher them on long tables. We had a smokehouse for the hog meat, which was salted down, and sometimes worms burrowed small holes in the meat, but we just trimmed the tainted meat and cooked it.

Momma made our soap by boiling fatback in a big steel pot all day, then adding lye and waiting for the bubbles to rise to the surface. She allowed it to cool, creating an uneven bar called lye soap. I used this waxy bar of soap, and it smelled stinky. When I bathed in the metal tub in our kitchen, this soap made my skin dry, so I applied petroleum jelly to heal the dryness on my hands and legs.

There was no doctor when my sister and I got sick with measles in January 1952. There was snow on the ground, and we had to stay inside. I had a rash of red bumps on my stomach and crusty, red eyes. Mary had tiny bumps on her face and a cough. Momma gave us corn husk tea and rubbed petroleum jelly on our chests. She had a tall bottle of castor oil, which was bitter and thick—and she made me lick the spoon. It took about ten days before we regained our strength. As a child, I thought castor oil with its sharp taste was like a punishment. But Momma saw it as a natural remedy to any ailment.

2

School Days

MY BROTHERS, SISTER, and I went to school about six months out of the year. At 5:30 in the morning, I woke up to eat my biscuits and rice, and afterward, I walked to the Colored school in the woods with my sister, Mary.[1]

I remember the other kids making fun of me when I was six years old with two front teeth missing. After that, I kept my mouth closed as much as possible. But I was happy to be in the first grade.

There were usually twenty students attending school in that little schoolhouse. Miss Jenkins, our teacher, was strict—no cursing allowed, and you had to say, "Yes, ma'am" when answering a question. She taught my brothers, Alfred and Wardell, and my cousins too. My

---

[1] Our one-room schoolhouse was about a half-mile from our house. I was told by a person who lived on the plantation years ago that Rosenwald was the name of my schoolhouse. I assume my school was started by Julius Rosenwald, president of Sears Roebuck. With the help of Booker T. Washington of Tuskegee Institute to guide the program, he built schools in the South during segregation because of underfunding of education for African Americans. The plan started around 1938 and continued to fund school in the rural south for many years. Learn more: https://savingplaces.org/places/rosenwald-schools#.YVHogEbMLX2

sister really liked our teacher, but my brothers thought she favored the girls because they never got paddled. Miss Jenkins had us read Bible verses after we sang "My Country, 'Tis of Thee" to begin each morning. Our books usually had missing pages because white children had used them for years before they were handed down.

Miss Jenkins taught us from first to ninth grade: spelling, arithmetic, English, penmanship, and geography. (Mary really knew her multiplication tables, and she wrote well in cursive.) Our teacher paddled a couple of students several times a week, usually boys who asked a lot of questions about the homework, and then she'd tell them to stand in the corner for not knowing their lessons.

The classroom was usually noisy, and there weren't enough desks for everyone, so some of the students sat on broken chairs. In the winter, I was too cold to sit at my desk because of the cracks in the windows, so I stayed next to the wooden stove.

Miss Jenkins rented a room from our neighbors, Deacon Jones and his wife on the plantation. Many times, she stayed late at school to ensure that I learned my alphabet and my numbers. Even now, I still remember Miss Jenkins' warm smile. She'd also assist me in reading *Fun with Dick and Jane* with its illustrations of a white girl with blonde hair and a white boy playing in sand; this was the first book I learned to read. I could relate to the context and words on the pages but not to the white children playing in the sand. Because I was picking cotton and often hungry, I could not visualize playing in the sand.

Most days, Miss Jenkins brought an apple or a piece of cornbread for her lunch, which she ate at her desk. Usually, I was hungry all day, and I filled my stomach with water. One time, my teacher saw me looking at her red apple, and she cut off two slices for me. I sat at my desk to savor the sweet taste. I was so happy that afternoon in class.

During recess, I used the toilet in the outhouse, a wooden frame structure about five feet tall, which I dreaded using. The dirt floor had ants crawling in the corner and a hive of wasps, called yellow jackets, hanging by the door. I tried to wait to pee until I reached my home after school because the outhouse smelled like a dead rat, and I had observed snakes crawling in the bushes adjacent to the door. There wasn't any toilet paper, either, and I had to wipe my hands on green leaves.

Recess was the time to run with my friends and climb trees. I played hide-and-seek in the woods, and I had fun hiding behind the logs and stumps. Other times, I ran after the squirrels with my classmate Betty Lou. In the winter, my brothers had to chop wood with an ax during recess with the other boys at school for our wood heater to keep us warm.

One rainy Friday morning in October as we walked to our schoolhouse, Mary and I passed our church, Mount Union, where we attended Sunday school every week. The church with a cross atop of it sat on cement blocks, and it adjoined the graveyard with its faded tombstones. I thought I saw the likeness of Deacon Shake, a man who had been dead for two years. The deacon had a white beard, and he used to bring peanut brittle candy for my friends and me. That day I saw his image with his hands stretched out at the church door. I wondered if this ghost was going to follow my sister and me. My granny had told us, "Ghosts get restless in their graves."

There were broken tombstones among the thicket bushes and stumps that lay in our path to school. My feet were wet from stepping into mud-holes, and I held Mary's hand tight because I thought I heard a whooshing sound from the heavy winds—I was sure someone was following us. I trembled as I held onto Mary's hand. By the time we got to school, my jacket and pants were soaked and my clothes were stuck to my thin body.

That morning I ran into the one-room schoolhouse. The heater was burning hot, and I hurried to stand in front of it with my sister. My hands were trembling. I never did feel warm or safe that day. I didn't even remember the lesson because I was cold, and my stomach ached. In the afternoon, my brother Wardell picked me up and carried me home to Momma wrapped in a blanket.

3

My Brother Alfred

I REMEMBER A RAINY afternoon in 1952 when two white army sergeants stepped onto our porch and knocked on the broken screen door. Daddy opened the door, and one of the men said, "Your son, Alfred Sims, was killed in action in Korea."

Daddy's voice quivered as he asked the soldier, "How did he die?" One of the soldiers handed my dad a brown envelope. On April 2, 1952, my twenty-two-year-old brother had been fighting in a segregated unit and was killed on the battlefield in Korea. His unit had been hit by a mortar shell.

Daddy yelled for my mom, my sister, and me. My mom knew it was bad news when she saw the soldiers. And when Daddy told her that Alfred had been killed, I remember my mom's piercing scream of "My son is dead!" She fainted onto the wood floor. Daddy rushed to pick her up in his arms and carried Momma to their bedroom to make sure that she was all right. Later, when Momma woke up, she was screaming and waving her arms.

Mary had been in the kitchen with me making cornbread, and as she listened to Daddy tell her about Alfred, she held her hands over her face while she cried. "My big brother won't be coming back to the plantation" was all she said. Then she pulled my thin body to her and rocked me in the squeaking rocking chair. I said, "Mary, I want to see my brother!" She continued to rub my back, saying, "Sis, it's gonna be all right."

With watery eyes, Daddy left the house to tell his brother, Uncle Roosevelt, and his wife, Aunt Mary, who lived on "The Quarters." They ran half a mile to our house with their children to be with us in our sorrow.

The neighbors had heard my mom's wailing screams. Soon members from Mount Union Church arrived at our house for an impromptu prayer vigil. Our small house was filled with people crying and telling stories of Alfred singing in the choir and how he helped our neighbors plow their gardens. In the meantime, the church folks brought plates of fresh-cooked neck bones with turnip greens, blueberry pies, and mason jars with canned apples. The church gave Daddy money to help with buying a plot for my brother at the Odd Fellows Rest cemetery in Aberdeen, the Colored cemetery that my Daddy would manage years later.

I just cried for hours while grasping the gold locket my brother had given me before he left on the train for Korea. I remembered how much Alfred liked swinging me around over his muscular shoulders. And how I'd yelled with laughter when he did it because I was only six years old.

Darkness became my world. I sat in my momma's lap for hours while she continued to moan. I remember thinking, *Why?*

Etta Mae, my best friend, spent the night with me. She was my classmate at school, and she could usually get me to smile by tickling me. I was usually happy, but not after my brother's death. I did not speak a word for days, and I just kept staring at the wall. I remember all the hugs and tears from family and friends, yet I was in my own world. I fed the chickens and helped my sister in the kitchen, but I was in a daze. I valued my friendship with my brother. I missed him so much, and I did not understand my feeling of anger and sadness. I kept thinking about how much Alfred had meant to our family.

My dad had not wanted Alfred to go to Korea because of the racism in the military and fearing he might not come back alive. Daddy trusted him, and the previous summer he had allowed Alfred to visit his Uncle Admiral in Chicago for the season. When Alfred returned to the farm, he was dressed in a fancy suit and a wide-brimmed hat, and he walked with his head in the air; he had confidence and faith in his beliefs. Alfred was ready for a change and feeling secure. He told Momma and Daddy about Chicago, and for the first time in his life, he felt a sense of freedom.

In the city, Alfred had seen Colored folks owning their homes and dressed in fine clothes in church. I remember my brother talking about the city life and the men driving new cars, and there were no wagons or cotton fields. I was happy to listen to his tales about Chicago. Soon after his return from that trip, he was drafted into the military.

Daddy wanted Alfred to stay out of the service because he was good at fixing the roof of the barn. Also, he enjoyed being with his sons in the field.

In 1951, after many conversations on the front porch with my brother about the Korean War, Daddy told him, "Son, you will be in a separate unit with other Colored soldiers just supporting the white troops, driving a truck, or cooking in the kitchen." Still, Alfred was enthusiastic about going into the army. My brother wanted to take care of our family and prove that Colored soldiers deserved to be treated as equals. It took years, but the army has changed to respect all veterans, and I wish my brother could have witnessed the diversity in today's military.

Alfred had planned to marry his sweetheart, Amelia, who was twenty-one years old. Before he left for Korea, Alfred brought Amelia, who was from Okolona, Mississippi, to dinner one Sunday to introduce her to the family, and she told my parents that she wanted to spend her life with Alfred. He had bought her an engagement ring, which sparkled on her finger. Alfred told us that they would get married when he returned from Korea. I don't remember much about her now except that she had long, black curly hair on her shoulders and wore a light-blue sundress. She and Alfred kept smiling at each other at the dinner table. They looked vibrant and happy together.

My brother Alfred was twenty-one years old when he took this picture with his girlfriend, Amelia. He was tall like Daddy, with broad shoulders and walnut-brown skin, and he liked telling jokes. His girlfriend had an oval face with high cheek bones, light brown skin, long, cascading hair on her shoulders, and a beautiful smile. Alfred was drafted into the army in 1951. The couple, who had met years earlier, wanted to get married when he left the army. Sadly, he was killed on the battlefield in Korea in 1952. Alfred always wanted a better life for our family, and I think he would have been proud to know that his life insurance money paved the way for us to leave the plantation and fulfill his dream for our us. I will never forget the sacrifice that he made for his country and our family.

My brother Wardell wasn't happy about their news at first. He eventually warmed up to the idea of his older brother getting married, but it took a while. These guys were a team. Wardell wanted his brother to be happy, but he would miss them hunting deer and rabbits and sharing memories of their childhood. Then, when Wardell met Amelia, all his doubts disappeared. He wanted his brother to be content.

Alfred Sims was only twenty-two years old when he died. Years later, when I saw Alfred's Purple Heart displayed in our living room, I realized that he gave the ultimate sacrifice for our family. With the government insurance money from his death, we were able to move to a new home in Aberdeen. My family was finally released from the ties of sharecropping.

4

Our New Life in Town

⁓ ❧ ⁓

THINGS CHANGED AFTER my brother Alfred's death. He had only been gone for three months, and now our lives would never be the same.

One day, my dad told me he had purchased a home in Aberdeen, and we were moving to town. I would miss my school friends, but I was thrilled to leave the plantation. Our family finally had momentum toward a better life.

In 1952, when I was seven years old, we moved to the small town of Aberdeen, which had a population of about five thousand people. Our house was on the Colored side of town. My parents bought the land, tore down the old house on the property, and built a new house with two bedrooms and modern appliances.

On moving day, my sister and I sat on the back of Deacon Wilson's faded green truck, where we were surrounded by cardboard boxes, broom handles, and pillows. Leaving our home on "The Quarters," the wooden frame house with a leaky tin roof, to move to Aberdeen was a blissful moment. I rode on the back of a rustic pickup truck with my sister, Mary. As the old truck passed Mr. Gilling's two-story house with a white picket fence, I thought this man had gotten rich from our labor and was living a privileged life. Finally, my family was free from the threat of losing our home and laboring for pennies a day.

In 1953, I was eight years old. I had recently moved to 308 Matubba Street, and my momma registered me at Vine Street Elementary School, which was two blocks from home. This school was in a new building with an inside toilet, and I sat in an auditorium to eat a warm lunch. I had two teachers and a desk that wasn't broken. Still, our books were used and torn. I was shy and barely opened my mouth to talk to my classmates. This transition was hard at first.

After a thirty-minute ride (that seemed much longer) on the gravel road in the sizzling heat, the deacon's truck pulled into the driveway of our new home at 308 Matubba Street. My parents had made several trips to Aberdeen to pick out this spot. It was a white house on the top of a hill, with green shutters and asbestos shingles.

Our new home was located between two wooden frames homes with daffodil flowers in the yard. On the left side of the house was a majestic magnolia tree with wide green, leathery leaves. I was excited as I jumped out of the truck, barefooted and wearing my overalls. Our next-door neighbor waved at me, and I learned from Momma that her name was Lucinda. That afternoon, she knocked on our front screen door wearing a blue apron and carrying a Mississippi Mud pie to welcome us to the neighborhood. It had a mountain of gooey chocolate on top with a crumbly crust. My eyes lit up with joy, and I thanked Miss Lucinda.

My house at 308 Matubba Street. I was a little girl living on the plantation when my family purchased our home in 1952, a little house with white paint and black shutters that sat on a hill with green grass and a magnolia tree in the yard. I often sat on the front porch in those two green chairs with my momma. My home was a place where I could sit and write on the pages of the Sear, Roebuck & Co. catalog about how, when Momma wasn't looking, I dipped my fingers into the batter for the cupcakes we were making for my seventh birthday. Once I moved away, I knew I could always come home when things got hard.

Estell, my momma, had arrived earlier. She wore a flowery apron with pockets for her keys, and she greeted us with hugs as we arrived. She smiled, showing her two gold teeth. As she opened the screen door of our new home, I detected the smell of fresh paint. I ran from room to room, excited to see my fancy new home. I looked around the kitchen and marveled at the metal sink with running water, a new white stove, and a GE refrigerator with a pitcher of cold water inside. The next stop was Momma's bedroom, which was light blue, and then on to the pale-green living room with its fancy white curtains covering the windows. Momma opened the door to my room, which was decorated with pink ruffled curtains that reminded me of the pictures I'd seen in *Look* magazine. On the farm, my room had muted colors and frayed curtains and a squeaky floor, but this new room had beautiful, shiny linoleum floors. I danced around the bedroom wearing a wide grin. I thought to myself, *I will be waking up with the sun shining in my room.*

Momma prepared a Sunday dinner after we moved to town and invited our family to share in the celebration of our new home. Uncle Jason and Uncle Curley, my dad's brothers, and Aunt Gracie, my mother's sister, and cousins from south of town brought barbeque ribs, watermelons, bottles of Coca-Cola, and sponge cakes, and I got to taste my first Jell-O with fruit salad.

Wardell, my dad, got a job as a janitor at city hall. His paycheck was just twenty dollars a week, so he picked up an extra job painting people's homes and setting up flower gardens in their backyards. He usually got paid with cash, but the white people who lived in large two-story houses paid him fifty cents an hour. The wages were cheap in 1955. Sometimes, he never received any money. If Daddy had complained, he would have been denied earning a living for our family. He had to pretend like he was satisfied to keep working.

Daddy was a man of few words, but he was always giving money to strangers in our community who were hungry. When I asked,

"Who is that man?" his response was usually, "I don't know him." That puzzled me because I was young, and I did not comprehend helping other needy folks.

Daddy sat on the back porch with his cat, Smokey, who had thick, gray fur and always followed Daddy to our garden. In the summertime, Daddy enjoyed purchasing a six-pack of Coca-Cola and sharing it with his brother Curley, who lived around the corner. Daddy worked six days a week from five o'clock in the morning until eight o'clock at night. He was like the mailman: the weather never stopped him from walking to work. He got up early on Sunday mornings, and he listened to the Rev. C. L. Franklin (father of singer Aretha Franklin) on the radio and then dressed up in his blue suit and Stetson hat for church at Daniel Baptist in Aberdeen, about a mile from the house. Daddy never owned a car; he walked four or five miles a day to church and his jobs. He continued to walk to work until he was ninety years old, and he never made any excuses. He just rose in the morning with the sunshine and read his Bible every day.

Daddy always kept a shotgun under his bed, both when we lived on the plantation and in this home, the only one he ever owned. He never showed any fear of the police while we lived on the plantation or when we lived in town. Since he worked at the city hall, he knew the officers at the precinct. He also knew the police chief, so he helped get young teenagers out of jail for minor offenses, and he took letters to inmates in jail from their families.

∽

In 1955, when I was around ten years old, Daddy got shingles, a painful rash that causes blisters that itch and affect the nerves; the outbreak was around his waist. He was bedridden for two weeks. A drove of people came to visit him, including my Uncle Roosevelt and Uncle Jason. Dr. Woodruff, the only Black doctor in town, treated

Daddy in the bedroom with the window open and a rotating fan on the chifforobe (a piece of furniture that combines a long closet for hanging clothes with a chest of drawers). I heard Momma tell Daddy's brother Curley Sims that he might die if the shingles rash made a full circle around his stomach. I told Mary, and we began crying and whimpering in the kitchen while washing the dishes. When we finished, I went into Daddy's room, where he was stretched out on the wooden bed gripping the sheets.

He was just staring at the ceiling with his long feet hanging off the end of the tall bed. I entered his room, tears rolling down my cheeks, and sat in the rocking chair by his bed. This was the first time that I could remember my dad being sick. He had on striped pajamas, and I saw a thick rash around his waist. I moved slowly to the bed and held his hand, and he put his wide arm around me. "Sis, what are you doing today?" he asked. I was at a loss for words. I simply nodded and gazed at him; I was so emotional that I could not speak. I left the room with my head tilted to keep from crying. Later, I just sat beside his door while Momma went in and out to nurse him. Afterward, I went to our garden and sat in the rows of corn stalks with Spooky, and I asked God to heal my dad because he was my whole world. After three weeks, Daddy returned to work at city hall. Life was back to normal.

∽

Daddy would often surprise my sister and me and cook us lunch. He baked pork chops with gravy and rice with cabbage and rutabaga. He poured us chocolate milk from the Piggly Wiggly grocery store on Maple Street. We gobbled down our meal with red hot peppers at the kitchen table, and a few flies swarmed around our plates.

My dad paid attention to my clothes. One time he took me shopping for a dress for church at Lasky's on Commerce Street. When I stepped out to model one with a low-cut neckline, Daddy looked at me and shook his head, so I knew he did not approve of that dress. He wasn't soft with his children, but he wasn't harsh either. He called me Sis, and my family still calls me Aunt Sis today.

On the other hand, my mom was strict and kept a tight rein on our behavior. She wore her colorful Sunday dresses and wide hats when we went to Pilgrim Rest Missionary Baptist Church, which was three blocks from home. I can still smell her Avon perfume, "Topaz"; I always looked forward to her dabbing a little behind my ear.

If I talked back to my momma, she went to the oak tree in the backyard and got a long switch to whip me. She had a hard time catching me because I ran from the kitchen to the bedroom, and I'd scream. If Daddy was home, he would not allow my mom to whip me. Momma continued to whip me until I was sixteen years old. I did not talk to her for days until she bought me a new dress.

During these years, I asked my momma about dating boys. Her answer was always, "Go to your room." I loved my momma, but I did not understand her whipping me or refusing to answer my questions about boys at my school. I suppose she thought she was protecting me.

Even though she was living in town, Momma still had her chickens in the backyard in a small hen house that my dad had built for them. That left me to do the chores of feeding seven hens and a rooster who had crusty feet and grabbing the eggs out of the nest. Momma kept me busy when she was off from work. I remember digging holes near the porch to plant azaleas and tulips. I watered the flowers, and I made sure the leaves were healthy. Occasionally, a small snake raised its head from under the bushes, and I screamed. Quickly, I'd grab the hoe and beat it in the grass. I was so scared; I think the snakes always slithered away.

Momma kept me busy in the yard or cutting okra from the stalks in the garden at 6:00 a.m. before she left for work; she was a nanny for a white lady. She cared for a baby girl and her brother, and she walked to and from the job. Sometimes Momma did not get paid her salary or got paid half of it. This was a common practice in those days; white people needed Black people for cheap labor, but they resented having to pay them.

Mary had a job too; she liked babysitting for two little white girls and preparing their lunch. We wanted to be productive like our parents and have our own allowances.

When I was fourteen years old in the summer of 1959, I worked on Franklin Street for the white family who owned the laundromat. The job was located three blocks from my home. Momma knew the lady, whose name was Miss Margaret; she was a brunette and had rebel flag tattoos on her arms. The job was part-time for three days a week in their home. Her husband, Randy, wore a greasy white cap and drove a red pickup truck with the Confederate flag and his bulldog in the back of the truck. My tasks around the modest, two-bedroom home were washing dishes, wiping windows, and feeding their bulldog, Lucky, who was stocky and had brown fur. I think he liked me because he followed me around the house.

Usually I made my own lunch, which was a peanut butter sandwich, wafers, and a tall glass of water. I was told to eat at the small metal table near the window. Lucky sat by me, panting and waiting for a snack. In the middle of the kitchen, Miss Margaret would drink her sweet tea while her husband puffed on a Marlboro cigarette at the square table. On the counter, the silver radio played music by Jerry Lee Lewis and the news. After a couple of days, I observed Margaret putting my plate and glass under the cabinet with the rat traps after I finished eating. I scratched my head, thinking, *Did she put my plate with the rat traps? I think that's a little strange.*

After I'd been working there for about two weeks, they turned on the small black-and-white Zenith television to the news one afternoon. I noticed a broadcast about a sit-in going on in Greensboro, North

Carolina. African American students were protesting at Woolworth, a retail chain that had a whites-only lunch counter. The students refused to leave the counter in the restaurant even though they were denied service. They continued to protest segregation, an action that was organized by the Student Executive Committee for Justice. At fifteen years of age, I was inspired to see that they were brown like me, protesting inequality and refusing to back down.

Randy stood in the kitchen with the television blasting, smoking his cigarettes. He said, "I don't know why these agitators are making trouble for our n*****rs in Mississippi."

My body was tense as I wiped the kitchen counter, and I recall gritting my teeth. I was thinking, *He is callous and irrational.* I walked outside to cool off. While looking at the clouds, I prayed to God for him to recover from the hate that I witnessed. At five o'clock, I left that house and ran home. I concluded, *Miss Margaret and her husband do not like me, and I don't feel safe around them.*

First, I told Momma that Miss Margaret had put my plate under the cabinet with the roach spray and that she bleached the toilet seat in the bathroom after I used it. With her hands on her hip, Momma told me to "quit that damn job." She finished our conversation with, "And I thought that woman was a Christian."

I dialed Miss Margaret's number and said, "I quit, and yesterday was my last day." She responded, "I tried to help you people," and then she slammed the phone down. The next day I stayed home to plant rose bushes in the yard with Momma, and I enjoyed watching the orange marigolds that attracted the butterflies.

Margaret called my mom, saying, "I don't know why your daughter left this job. I paid her good, and she had thirty minutes for lunch." Momma responded, "Thank you, but I want my daughter to stay home for the summer."

I kept wondering about the behavior of this woman and her moral values as a human being. I was confused about her attitude. This was the first time I had shared a space with a white family. I was learning about the racial attitudes that separated us in Aberdeen. It made me feel unequal and irritated.

5

Our Life in the South

I WENT TO TOWN with my sister on Saturday morning to do some shopping. We'd saunter down the rock road past the antebellum home and oak trees. After twenty minutes, we were on Main Street passing the Elkin Theatre. I never went there, but I am told that the white folks sat downstairs and the Colored folks sat upstairs. Around the corner, the smells from Kimmel Bakery drifted from the door, so we'd stop for the best-tasting cinnamon rolls in town, made from scratch by a German baker. Next, we'd cross Commerce Street with its one red light, and Mary would hold my hand like I was a little kid.

Soon, we'd be standing in front of the V. J. Elmore store, which we called the Dime Store. Mary led the way in through the front glass doors, and after I spent some time looking at the toys on the shelf, I decided on a bag of Hot Tamales and Hubba Bubba gum. Then I'd realized I was thirsty … but even quenching my thirst was a race-related event.

I always looked forward to going into town with my sister on Saturdays. At Elmore's Dime Store, Mary and I would stroll to the water fountains in the back of the store, which had big signs that read WHITE ONLY and COLORED. The water fountain for whites was modern with cool water and a shiny faucet. Mary and I drank from the water fountain for Colored, which was rusty with a dingy sink, and the water was warm. I did ask my sister about the separate fountains, but she just tightened her lips … no response. This was one of the many symbols of the divide in the South.

As we left leaving the dime store, the cashier smiled at a little white girl, but she frowned at me when I looked at her.

I heard on the radio that Colored folk needed to know their place. The words were hard for me to understand. Even at eight years old, I wondered why I felt isolated. When I looked in the mirror, I saw a girl with braided hair, thick hips, and a wide nose. Momma told me I was pretty, but I did not like my reflection in the mirror, and I was bashful. I wanted to visualize that one day I might look and feel beautiful like the models in *Ebony* magazine.

My Uncle Jason Sims, my dad's younger brother, worked at Hussey, a general store owned by brothers C. L. and Eddie Hussey. Uncle Jason was a butcher; he was the only Colored person I knew who worked in a job where he was not carrying a broom or a mop, and he was one of few Negroes who worked in the stores in town as a butcher.

Older people got their government checks on the first of the month, and they cashed them at Hussey because they got credit from the brothers who owned the store. Many of these people were illiterate, and they signed their names with an X. Some were field hands from Prairie, Mississippi, a small town with one stoplight, who came into town from picking cotton on the plantation. Their trip to Hussey was probably the first time in a while that they had inhaled the scent of something other than a mule or cotton being loaded onto a wagon.

Hussey had one entrance for whites, and Colored people entered the store through a side door and sat in the back. It was the only store in town where a Colored person could sit and rest on a bench, where they could drink RC cola and dig into BBQ ribs or a sandwich of hog head cheeses and a cup of ice cream. Many of the customers would sit on sacks of flour or boxes because there weren't any tables, and they dipped Peach Sweet snuff or Brown's Mule chewing tobacco. And the smoke from cigars and Lucky Strike cigarettes often got so thick that it looked like fog.

One of the happiest moments there for me in Hussey was seeing the smiling face of my Uncle Jason at the counter, and of course he handed me a lollipop. He called me "Boy" because he had five boys, and I knew how to box the guys and jump on their backs in the yard. I didn't mind rolling in the dirt.

My dad had credit at Ernest Westbrook's grocery on Vine Street down the road from my home. He was outgoing and friendly and gave credit to his neighbors. Daddy got credit at the store for me. After school, I took my best friends to the store for Bazooka bubble gum and Jolly Ranchers. Soon, my dad got the bill. Daddy shouted, "What happened at Westbrook's store?" I told him I just wanted to have fun with my friends. Daddy pursed his lips tight like he'd just eaten a lemon. He yelled, "No more credit, you hear me, Sis?" I felt so bad, and I told him, "I am sorry, Daddy, that I messed up." As I gazed at him with my sad eyes, he reached over and hugged me.

Occasionally when we were at Hussey, we bumped into Momma's friend from Mount Nebo church, our cousin Sister Etta Mae. She wrapped her long arms around my skinny shoulders, and with snuff under her bottom lip, she laid a kiss on my forehead. I frowned because I felt that wet spit sticking to my forehead. There was a Colored bathroom in town, but it had a dirt floor with one dim light, so I didn't want to go there to get the spit off. When Sister Etta Mae walked away, I said, "Momma, get this nasty stuff off my head." Momma quickly found a handkerchief to wipe the spit off my head. I just wanted to rush home to take a bath!

I was getting an allowance at nine years old, and I used it to buy pork skin rinds and candied lemon slices at Westbrook, which I'd walk to on the gravel road with my sister, Mary. I was happy deciding what candy to purchase at the store and being with my sister, who thought she knew everything since she was the oldest. In the sixth grade, my candy of choice was Sugar Daddy, a thick caramel on a stick. It was sweet and hard, and I cracked my tooth on that candy at school.

ᴄ❍

Summertime was the best season of the year, and we invited our friends to hang out with us while Momma was working. I'd just had my ninth birthday, and my sister was fifteen years old. On our school vacation, we played loud music on the radio: we heard the popping sounds of Elvis Presley's "Hound Dog" and the groovy sounds of Lloyd Price singing "Stagger Lee." I was always dancing barefooted in the mirror in my blue jeans. Of course, I was pretending that I was on stage at Shivers High. I drank red Nehi sodas and chewed on pigs' feet and got greasy juice on my hands. And my sister had her crunchy pork skin rinds from the Westbrook grocery store, which was a block away. I had chores to do in the kitchen, but this was our playtime.

Those happy times were often overshadowed by darker events like my cousin being arrested.

One day in 1954, when I was eight years, I remember sitting in the living room on our green leather sofa. It was thundering, and the wind was blowing on the windowpane. Momma chewed Brown's Mule tobacco, and her green spittoon sat next to the couch. With a solemn tone in her voice, she told me about the Klan, a white supremacist group that wore white hoods and robes to "keep social order" and prevent Colored people from voting. Our neighbor Old Man Jimmy had his arm broken by the police for trying to register to vote at city hall. Momma said they had burned a cross at her friend's home on the south side of town. She told me, "They hate us Negros, and they believe that we are a threat to their race." I asked her, "Are the Klan members coming to our home?"

"No," she told me. "Don't worry, your dad knows what to do to keep us safe." Momma clenched her hands in her apron pocket.

⌒

I had a cousin named Bobby McMillian, who we called Boog. He lived with my Aunt Gracie on Forest Street near the cemetery. Boog was tall with broad shoulders. He would visit us on Saturdays for breakfast to eat my momma's fluffy biscuits with sorghum molasses and play with my dog, Spooky.

Bobby was just nineteen years old and lived on the south side of town when he was arrested for allegedly raping a white woman who lived in the area. There was no physical evidence to link him to the crime in any way. My dad tried to get him a lawyer, but no one in town would take his case. While he was in jail awaiting trial, he was beaten and denied bail. I pleaded with my daddy to help Boog, but he told me none of the white attorneys would take his case.

After three months, he was sentenced by an all-white jury to serve twenty years at the maximum-security Mississippi State Penitentiary, also known as Parchman Farm. Elizabeth McMillian, his mom who lived in New York, did get him a lawyer from New York, but it was too late to help him because he had been sentenced already.

Parchman Farm was the same prison where the late civil rights activist, Freedom Rider, and US Representative John Lewis, would be imprisoned in 1961 for thirty-seven days for using a "whites only" bathroom.

My mom, my sister, and I went to visit Boog in prison. I was ten years old, and this was three months after he had been sentenced. Before I entered the prison gate, I saw a tall lookout tower with guards holding shotguns. Once we were inside the prison, the guards tore apart the package of pork ribs, beans, biscuits, and the chocolate cupcakes that my momma had brought for Boog. Tears welled in my eyes when I saw the thick iron chains around his bruised ankles, and he was so skinny with a shaved head. He told me that he picked cotton and soybeans in the 100-degree weather and only got one meal a day. I imagine that a wild animal got treated better than my cousin.

After fifteen years of incarceration for a crime he did not commit, Boog was released from prison, but he was not the same person who had gone into that prison, and he died six months later. In 1956, there was no DNA evidence to prove a man's innocence, nor a group like the Innocence Project to fight for him. This was a grave injustice. Even in 2021, one-third of the prisoners in our jails are Black men; this is a grave injustice. I am still wary of the justice system.

6

My Visit to the Doctor

N O INTERACTION WITH white people was free of bigotry in those days. One night in July of 1957, I had a stomach problem and threw up in my bed on my yellow pillow. Mom made me drink that nasty corn husk tea again, to make me feel better. At six o'clock the next morning, the skies were cloudy, but it was still 97 degrees. Momma, who was barely five feet tall, banged on the wall of my room and commanded, "Sis, get out of bed." Then she peeked her head around the door and asked, "Is your stomach still aching"? I said, "I still feel nauseous." Momma came into my room and sat on the floral quilt on my bed. She whispered in my ear, "I'm taking off from work to take care of you."

Momma usually woke me up with a belt and barking orders for me to feed the chickens in the hen house, but she was humming that morning. In the kitchen, the radio played Mahalia Jackson belting out, "He's Got the Whole World in His Hands." And Momma was clapping her hands.

With a toothpick in her mouth and a green bonnet on her head, she dialed the phone to call Miss Judy, her boss lady. I listened as

Momma told her, "I ain't coming to watch your chillen or scrub the floors today because my daughter is sick." I could hear Miss Judy's angry voice on the other end; she called my momma Esther instead of Estell and told her, "Start walking to my house, and be there by seven a.m." Momma replied, "My name is Estell Sims, and I have a home on Matubba Street." She hung up the phone and turned to me. "You know what that hussy said?" Momma sighed. "She shouted, 'You are fired.' That red-headed woman has the devil in her this morning. My baby girl comes first."

Momma grabbed the rotary phone again and called Jimmy Lee, our neighbor, to drive us to the doctor before he started working in his garden. At 7:45 a.m., he pulled up to our front steps in his green Ford with its cracked windshield, and asked, "How y'all doing today, Mrs. Sims?"

Mom sat in the front seat and rolled down the window. I sat in the back seat and caught a whiff of pee. I held my nose while the old truck rattled past the elegant antebellum homes. After a couple of miles, Jimmy Lee stopped in front of the doctor's building on Hickory Street. "Much obliged, Jimmy," Momma said after we exited the vehicle.

The sign hanging out front of the clinic read COLORED ONLY in bold, white letters. The paint on the building was peeling. Sleeping in front of the office was a brown-and-white collie that reminded me of Lassie on television. I thought that dog might bite me, so I nudged his head with my foot and said, "Wake up!" He rolled over, got up, and hobbled to the oak tree. Momma mumbled, "That dog is old, and didn't you see his front leg is missing?" No, I didn't notice, but I hoped someone was taking care of that puppy.

Momma held my hand, her money pouch tucked in her bosom, and I turned the rusty doorknob to enter. Wiping sweat with my handkerchief, I walked into the waiting room, which had faded wallpaper and a padded couch with unraveling threads. The lone window was propped open, and flies swarmed around freely. As we sat and waited, sweat rolled down my momma's cheeks. Soon, a young girl with a blue blouse slid open the glass window at the counter and shouted, "Hi y'all, who needs to see the doctor?"

"My daughter, Estell, is sick."

"Y'all got money to pay for this?"

"Yessum."

She handed Momma a notebook with some forms and a pencil. "Do you know how to read?" she asked. When Momma said she did, the woman pointed to the couch we'd been sitting on and told us, "Sit down over there." We waited for two hours before the door swung open, and a tall nurse who wore big, ugly white shoes called, "Estell Sims." I hopped off the old couch, and the nurse said, "My name is Miss Maribelle."

In the hallway, Nurse Maribelle told me to "Step on the scale, little girl." I weighed eighty pounds. Then, we followed Nurse Maribelle to the exam room, and she asked, "What is wrong this child?"

Momma told her I had pains in my stomach. The nurse said loudly, "Put the girl on the table and open her dress."

The exam table was cold and covered in plastic, and the smell of alcohol assaulted my nostrils; the paint on the walls was flaking. Nurse Maribelle slammed the door as she left the room, and the glass door shook. I asked my momma what was wrong. Shaking her head, Momma laid her hand on my head and said, "You are going to be fine, baby!"

Dr. Carson entered the exam room wearing a short, white jacket with a stethoscope around his neck. He was around sixty-five years old and had peppery gray hair, and he walked with a limp. In a slow, Southern drawl, he said, "Hello, Estell. I see that your daughter is sick." Momma responded that I had an upset stomach and was throwing up. Dr. Carson lightly touched my stomach and asked me if I was in pain. "No, sir," I told him.

When he had finished his exam, the doctor turned back to my mom. "I will get the nurse to give her a shot. I think this girl has a virus." Dr. Carson called for the nurse, and when she didn't appear, he shouted again. Finally, she entered the room; her red face and thin-lipped grimace made it clear she unhappy to be back in the room, and she stood near the open window. The doctor told her, "Give Estell a shot," and the nurse turned her back to us. She marched out of the room and slammed the door, again.

Momma said, "Doctor Carson, what is wrong with that nurse? She won't touch my child." Momma's whole body trembled with anger as she clutched her beige hat. I stood at the foot of the exam table and stared at the blades of the fan rotating on the counter. My heart pounded in my chest. Shaking his head, the doctor gave me the shot in my arm.

When he'd finished, Dr. Carson said, "Some folks just don't like you people."

Shocked and full of rage, Momma said, "Damn you, you righteous, ignorant fool." I was scared for Momma. We left the exam room and bolted past the front desk. Momma and I moved so fast that I lost one of my sandals. As we hurried past, the cashier hollered, "Aren't you going to pay your bill?" Momma said, "Hell, no! The nurse acted like my child had a disease."

I feared for Momma that the doctor might call the police, and she would go to jail. Once we were in the parking lot, I asked her, "What's wrong with me?"

"The nurse did not want to touch your dark skin," Momma said and then added, "You are better than these hypocrites, you're Estell."

For years afterward, I would not go to a doctor in Aberdeen, and I still wonder to this day if I am being treated the same as everyone else. The incident with the nurse that demoralized me while I was sick has stuck with me all these years.

7

My Teenage Years

~~~~~~

L IKE MOST YOUNG people, I was in a hurry to grow up. I
started Shivers High School in 1960, and it was fun because
I had two great friends, Lois and Elizabeth. We dressed alike,
and we were good-looking and smart, too. I liked wearing pink lipstick, and I got my hair straightened and curled like the other girls.
Momma got me a pair of white heels, and she bought my jackets and
shirts for school from Lasky's on Commerce Street. My brand-new
clothes lifted my self-esteem. I never wore a school uniform, but I
wore gingham skirts just below the knee.

At Vine Elementary School, I had fallen behind and my grades
were just mediocre, but when I entered Shivers High, I began to
understand concepts and set goals for doing my homework. I was
on the honor roll for the first time in the tenth grade. I was happy
to attend Shivers High School in the new brick building on Vine
Street, which was two blocks from my home. The old Colored high
school was a wooden building with broken windows near Franklin
Street. Around 1958, Shivers High School was built and dedicated
to an outstanding educator, my principal, J. R. Shivers. I remember

Principal Shivers sticking his head in the door to check on my history class. Although he was busy in the office, he cared about his students. He was a community leader and helped our parents raise money to buy my clarinet so I could play in the school band.

Momma bought a secondhand clarinet on layaway at the music store for me to learn to play. My reed often had a splinter, and it pricked my lips, but I still had to know my lessons in my music books, songs like "Twinkle, Twinkle, Little Star," which I played every day. Momma set a schedule for me to practice my clarinet on the porch because she couldn't stand the strange sounds coming from it.

The band wore dark blue uniforms that had been handed down from the white high school. Our band mothers raised money on the weekends by having a wiener roast and candied apple displays at the church, and Principal Shivers came to assist us. The school used this money to buy drums and music stands. Our band teacher, Mr. Bates, had been in the army, and he believed in discipline. None of us wanted to know what his strap felt like.

I continued to excel in my classes until I finished high school. My favorite class was English, and my teacher, Ms. Whitefield, went to my church, Pilgrim Rest. She is one of the people who helped me learn and appreciate writing. One thing I still remember is reading Walt Whitman's "O Captain, My Captain!" I had been writing short poems in my journal since I was ten years old, and the rhythmic pattern of the poem appealed to me. Colored poets like Paul Lawrence Dunbar, who wrote "We Wear the Mask," had been ignored in my literature books.

I was popular in high school, and I remember several of the boys. For instance, I recall sixteen-year-old Jerome, who lived down the street, smiling at me with his buck teeth. And Robert, my boyfriend at Shivers High School, was always writing me notes. He was six feet tall with a close-crop haircut and broad shoulders. Robert was on the football team, and he had eyes only for me.

Estell in high school. I turned sixteen in 1961. I had a new hairstyle, and my sister helped me look pretty with makeup. For this photo, I wore my momma's red lipstick and the necklace that Daddy bought me from Maier's Jewelry Store on Commerce Street. I was getting good grades; I was on the honor roll and excited about college. I was also daydreaming about traveling to a new city, like Chicago. I read *Ebony* and *Look* magazines, and I wanted to live in a place with tall buildings and a subway. I had known that I wanted to leave Aberdeen since I was twelve years old. I was curious about the world and meeting new people. I was tired of going to the back door of restaurants and stores, I deserve respect. I begin to visualize and close my eyes to imagine a new life with me going to college and owning a home like my parents.

Our school mascot was the Bearcats. For football games, I wore my blue band uniform that was missing a couple of buttons on the sleeve. After the football game, Robert walked me home and carried my books. He held my hand, and sometimes he sneaked a kiss on my front porch; I made sure Momma wasn't peeping out the door because I would have been in trouble. I guess you could say we were going steady. I told my friend Elizabeth Ann, "This guy thinks that I am special."

Robert took me to the Shivers High School prom; I felt special that night in my long, pink gown with pink ruffles and a matching pink wrist corsage that Robert had purchased. He was dressed in a fabulous tuxedo, and he drove us there in his red 1958 Ford sedan.

Colorful decorations and bright lights transformed the auditorium into a ballroom. I got my picture taken with my friends Lois and Elizabeth with my new Kodak camera. While mingling in the crowd, I was the best-looking girl at the prom. Although my white high heels were squeezing my toes, I was into the groove of the music. Then I began twirling around and twisting to the music of Chubby Checkers' song "The Twist" as it played on the record player.

Elizabeth told me, "You are a good dancer."

Laughing, I replied, "Oh girl, I was doing what I saw on *American Bandstand*."

I did settle down and drink some fancy green punch with slices of lemons. One of my classmates, Roxie, sneaked out of the building with her boyfriend, Paul Mackie. My classmates kept giggling about them kissing. Soon the chaperon, Miss Maybell, a tall woman with a big nose, was looking in the crowd for them. I suppose Maggie and her boyfriend had other plans.

The prom was over at 10:30 p.m., and Robert drove me home. I sneaked a kiss with Robert. I know my momma was peeping through the blinds, but this was my prom night!

My friend Elizabeth Ann came to spend the night with me on several Saturdays, and we talked about kissing boys and going on a date. We were simply daydreaming! We lived by the rules of the church to stay pure until marriage. When I was sixteen years old, Momma and I had a serious argument because I wanted to go to a drive-in movie with my friends. "No," she said firmly, "you are staying home with your sister."

I learned teamwork by practicing my music with my friends and traveling on the school bus to Starkville and Tupelo for concerts. We had chaperones on those trips who made us stay in our seats, and the girls sat in the back. I read comic books and drank warm Nugrape soda while munching on Twizzlers and Pixy Stix.

I enjoyed going to the girls' basketball games at Shivers High School and sitting on the bleachers with my classmates while cheering the team. After the game, my dad—people called him Mr. Wardell—picked me up at the front door of the building. I smiled when I saw my dad waiting for me after the basketball game. One time when he arrived at the gym, I was talking to my classmate Eddie. Daddy, who was six feet tall and wore black-rimmed glasses, had a frown on his face, and the boy rushed off. There were no words about this boy to me, but Daddy showed his attitude. All he said was, "Sis, are you ready to go home?" Yes, Daddy.

᳚

The first time I remember hearing my parents talk about Tuskegee Institute was when I was at Vine Street Elementary School in 1957. They told me about Booker T. Washington, the African American educator who in 1881 became the first president and principal developer of Tuskegee Normal and Industrial Institute, now called Tuskegee University, and recruited George Washington Carver, the agricultural chemist who developed many products for farmers, like peanuts, soybeans, and sweet potatoes. I had not been taught about these men in my history classes nor read about them in our Colored library.

Momma wanted me to be educated to find a good husband and be a housewife; that was the goal my parents had for me. Many weekends, Momma taught my sister and me how to sit in a chair like young ladies and walk with a book on our heads to improve our posture. My momma believed in proper etiquette for us so that we could meet the right people.

Although I got her message, I wanted to be independent. My ambition in life was to become an elementary school teacher. Moreover, I was looking forward to traveling because I was curious about other cultures. I had outgrown that small, segregated town. I wanted to conquer a new space. Even though I was somewhat scared, I knew for sure that it was my time. I intended to leave Aberdeen when I finished high school. Perhaps I would live in a big city like Chicago or New York.

While I was in the twelfth grade in January of 1963, Miss Whitfield, my English teacher, suggested that I send a letter to the registrar at Tuskegee. I had perfect attendance in high school for three years, and my transcripts were excellent; being on the honor roll added to my credibility. I thought that maybe I could feel valued as a person at Tuskegee. In March, I received my acceptance letter! When I told my parents the good news, Momma said, "My baby is going to college."

I worried about how I would afford to attend Tuskegee. God knows I didn't have any money. I worried about a scholarship or borrowing money for my tuition. I talked to Daddy while he sat in his rocking chair with his fuzzy-tailed cat, Mount. "I'll find a way for you to attend Tuskegee, Sis," he mumbled, and I knew if anyone could do it, Daddy would. I prayed each day for a miracle.

Daddy got a loan from the First National Bank for five hundred dollars for my tuition. I clutched Daddy's hand tightly when he shared the news that he had the money for my tuition; I was overwhelmed with joy. That Friday morning when I learned the news, my Uncle Curley, Daddy's brother, was visiting. He hugged me and said, "Sis, I trust you to do your best at Tuskegee."

My sister and I celebrated my acceptance to Tuskegee over her freshly made banana pudding at the kitchen table, with gospel music playing on the radio in the background. Mary had a new hairstyle with tight curls, and her smooth brown skin glowed. While we sat shoulder to shoulder at the table, she lamented, "I will miss staying up until five in the morning and nibbling on popcorn." And we laughed about how Daddy in his pj's would stick his head out of the bedroom and yell, "Y'all go to bed." We reminisced about the State Fair that came to Aberdeen every summer with the brightly colored Ferris wheel, where we would gobble down pink cotton candy that made our faces sticky. Daddy allowed us to roam around to see the clown and the fun-house mirrors at the fair. Once, in the barn area with the livestock, I got to milk a black-and-white cow, and it was messy.

When I graduated from Shivers High on May 29, 1963, I wore a white cap and gown and tall white heels. The auditorium was full of families standing in the aisles. I still remember hearing "Pomp and Circumstance" and marching past yellow flowers. Wobbling in my heels, with sweat rolling down my eyebrows, I stepped on the stage to get my diploma from Principal Shivers. My classmates cheered, "Go, Estell!" Underneath my robe, I wore a new pencil-style dress with lace and a pearl necklace, which boosted my confidence. And for my special day, Momma had purchased pink lipstick and perfume from Avon and new underwear from Sears and Roebuck, too.

I was so proud of my parents that day: Momma stepped out wearing her light-blue church hat with a matching dress, and Daddy looked elegant in his blue suit and striped tie. As we walked the three blocks from our home to the ceremony, Momma, whose lips were tight, cursed at Daddy about money. I hollered, "Momma, can you settle down, because this is my day." When I saw her startled look, I thought I might get slapped. However, she just stared and then flashed a smile that showed her gold teeth.

My mom and dad dressed up for my brother Wardell's wedding in Atlanta, Georgia, when I was in high school. This was the first time that Momma and Daddy had been out of town together, and they had a good time. I know they were the best-looking couple at the wedding.

My dad, Wardell Sims, is dressed in a black suit and one of the thin ties he preferred. My mother, who everyone called Mrs. Estell Sims, took pride in her looks and is dressed in white chiffon with a beaded necklace and a pillbox hat with a veil.

Then summer was over, and I packed my footlocker with pictures of my family and my red music box, a gift from my brother Wardell, who was away in college. Momma gave me her Bible, a gift from her momma, Mary Jane Pruitt, to take with me. She warned, "You need to talk to the Lord when things get rough, and you can always come home." "Yes, ma'am, I know," I told her. But thinking about leaving home for the first time and being on my own made me nervous. Who was going to look after me?

In August, Momma, Daddy, and I left Aberdeen for the three-hundred-and-fifty-mile drive to Alabama. Our neighbor, brother Wilson pulled into the beautiful campus of Tuskegee after driving us there in his old Ford. I couldn't control my excitement, and I began screaming, "I am finally at Tuskegee!" I couldn't believe I was there among the oak trees and neatly cut hedges and the big sign that read TUSKEGEE INSTITUTE. Later, the name changed to Tuskegee University. I checked into an old wood building, which was my dorm. I met my dorm mother at the front desk and signed papers, including one stating that I understood that guys were not allowed to visit our dorm rooms. I got keys to room #12, which had a rotating fan on a desk and one chair. The closet was adjacent to the bed, and the bathroom was down the hall. Daddy put my cardboard box of hot dogs, spicy wings, apples, and Hot Tamales candy on the wooden table. I hopped on the bed, and Momma began pulling my pants and shirts, toothbrush, and makeup out of the suitcase.

After I got settled in my dorm, my parents embraced me. Daddy said, "Sis, things will not be same without you at home. I'll take care of your dog, Spooky." With slumped shoulders, I shuffled down the hallway with my mom and dad to say goodbye. I stood on the porch of the dorm with my arms folded and watched as my parents climbed into the old sedan and waved. Then I slowly strolled back to my room, and I cried like I was twelve years old because it was my first move away from family and friends.

By morning, my eyes were puffy, yet I hopped out of bed and put on my red Tuskegee cap and my sneakers to visit the museum for the Tuskegee Airmen. They were the first Black military pilots in the US Army Air Corps (the predecessor of the US Air Force), and they trained at nearby Tuskegee Army Airfield. The African American military pilots from the 332nd Fighter Group helped the Allies win World War II. They were nicknamed "Red Tails" for their distinctive planes. Even though senior army leadership wasn't sure Blacks were "teachable" to fly airplanes, they proved that they could manage sophisticated aircraft. Indeed, they won hundreds of medals, and I was impressed by their courage.

Next, I saw the Carnegie Building; it was an old wooden building, and George Washington Carver probably had his science lab there all those years ago. Finally, I saw a statue of Booker T. Washington, who started this historic college with a dream for a better life for our people. These men emphasized education and self-reliance for young Black students like me.

I was excited to interact with students from Nigeria and the Caribbean on campus, getting to know other cultures. The campus was large; making friends seemed daunting. But I was determined to get involved and join the book club on campus. After standing in a long line with fifty other students at the administration building, I received my ID cards, and I was so proud … I was a Tuskegee student!

Soon I met my roommate, Carolyn, from Augusta, Georgia, who had lived on a farm too. Down the hall, I met Octavia from New York City, and she told me about shopping on Fifth Avenue in Manhattan. I was inspired by our chat. Many of the students in my building were from small towns in the South, and it was their first time leaving home too. They were homesick like me.

I learned the names of all the students in my building and spent many hours that semester studying with them. After class, I usually went to the cafeteria with my roommate, Carolyn. Both of us liked coconut cake. She talked about her twin brother, and I talked about my dog, Spooky, and how he would bark at the neighbors. In the cafeteria, the jukebox played "Take Five" by Dave Brubeck; that was a groovy jazz song. Carolyn introduced me to the cook, Betsy, who filled my plate with homemade rolls, pork chops, and sweet potato pie. This reminded me of Momma's cooking on a warm Saturday afternoon in Aberdeen.

The semester started in the middle of August. My schedule included math, biology, English, and history. Biology at Tuskegee was in a big room with risers and about 100 students. I sat in the front seat to take notes. At Shivers High School, my biology teacher, Mr. Thompson, had a small, noisy classroom with about forty-five students. I sat in the back of the classroom, and I thought biology was boring. But at Tuskegee, the biology professor showed us living organisms in jars, and there were microscopes with different lenses. I did an experiment on earthworms, and I wrote a lab report. Soon, I was able to use my knowledge from biology to find worms on the sidewalks near my dorm and allow them to crawl on my hands. Carolyn said, "I can't believe that you're touching those segmented worms." I was just curious about nature.

During the fall semester at Tuskegee, I had to take a remedial class in biology. I was frustrated that I was far behind the other students. The lab area offered a tutor, and I was introduced to Miss Johnson. This gray-haired lady grilled me like I was in elementary school, and I became motivated and eager to learn. I received a B in biology that semester.

For the first time, I realized that Shivers High School had lacked the resources to give me a quality education, and I was disappointed. Even though I'd made the honor roll in high school, there was a disparity in my education. I was ashamed that my college grades were poor, but I was determined to continue my education.

Tuskegee was a nurturing environment that helped to motivate me and inspired me to become a lifelong learner.

On campus during the week, I walked around in my loafers and cardigan. I often joined Carolyn after class, and we would go to the Tuskegee library, which had books on Latinx, Afro-American, and

European cultures as well as the classics. On the shelf, I saw Zora Neale Hurston's *Their Eyes Were Watching God*, which told about women finding their identity. And I could relate to that story.

I had fun on the Tuskegee campus on weekends. I dressed in my crimson and gold T-shirt because I was a fan of the football team, the Golden Tigers, and its team mascot, which we just addressed as "Hey there, Mr. Tiger!" When we played Alabama State, our players whumped their team. The cheerleaders with their red pom-poms and the band marching at halftime had me bubbling with excitement. I climbed the bleachers to buy popcorn, candied apples, and hard sour candy to share with friends from the guys in white hats who roamed the stands. I will never forget those joyous moments at the stadium on Friday nights.

During that time, my mom and dad sent me chocolate fudge candy from Kimmel's in Aberdeen, which filled my heart with joy. I knew I had to do well and make them proud.

One of the memorable times at Tuskegee was when I went to a concert to see my favorite idol, soul singer and dancer James Brown. The students roared with excitement. I was at the auditorium, wearing my new red sweater and a braided hairstyle, with thousands of other students. Brown sang, "Please, Please, Please," which I knew as "Please Don't Go" from singing along to this hit song on the radio. I saw him perform the signature routine, the Mashed Potato, with his electrifying dance moves. James Brown and his group The Famous Flames were dressed in flashy black suits. The image of my first time seeing a Black celebrity performing on stage is still etched in my memory.

In May of 1964, at the end of my freshman year, I returned to Aberdeen to stayed with my family for a month. I did not have money for the next semester, so I decided to get a job. Almost from the moment I arrived, I was determined to leave Aberdeen as soon as possible.

For years, I had vowed that I would move to the big city to get a sense of freedom. In July 1963, I bought my ticket for New York

City to visit my cousin and get a summer job. Two weeks later, I went to the Trailways bus station with my footlocker, luggage, and a box of cold fried chicken with potato salad. I was excited, but also sad to leave my family. Tears rolled my cheeks as I hugged my dad, momma, and Mary and said goodbye; I knew I would miss them.

I planned to return in time to go back to Tuskegee in the fall.

8

The Big Apple

IN JULY OF 1964, I stepped off the Trailways bus at the Port Authority terminal with sweat on my brow and ninety-eight dollars in my purse. Of course, I'd spent the entire three-day trip—more than 1,000 miles—seated in the back of the bus; the white folk sat up front. The driver, who had a Southern drawl, spoke in a loud and clear voice, "Negro seats are in the back."

I was unable to sleep because the seats were as comfortable as sitting in a metal chair. The bus stopped every three hours at some small-town depot. When I first got on the bus, I was reluctant to move my small luggage or speak to other passengers. As people got on and off the bus, a young lady with a lilac cap sat beside me. She chuckled and told me her name was Teresa. The scent of her drugstore perfume, Morning Glory, permeated the air, and it made me sneeze. She wore a yellow sundress and white sandals that showed off her big feet. When she began talking loudly to the older man across the aisle, she said, "I'm getting off the bus in South Carolina." I was relieved because, for a while, I could forget about being alone on a strange bus with its roaring noise as it sped up on the road.

While Tenesha and I rode together, I learned that she liked the Sam Cooke song "A Change Is Gonna Come" and loved to dance. (I enjoy moving my feet on the dance floor, but I am a little clumsy.) Meeting Tanesha kept me occupied, and her funny jokes made me giggle. The next morning, she had reached her destination. She embraced me and covered me with that scent before sauntering off the bus.

Next, we stopped in Washington, DC before going on to New York. I couldn't eat in the restaurant; I was still in the South. The signs that hung on the entrance were clear: WHITE ONLY. I had brought a brown paper bag with pork skins and a cinnamon roll. I also had bologna sandwiches and Vienna sausages with saltine crackers.

In DC, we got a new white driver who was friendly and unlike the other driver with his annoying, piercing eyes. After the new driver came on the bus, the back of the bus with the Colored folk was filled with loud talking and giggling. For most of the trip, I stared out the window and gazed at the green trees and the cumulus clouds. I also pulled out my journal to write about my Saturday afternoons with my sister and how the mosquitoes bit our legs while we sipped red Kool-Aid.

I daydreamed about when I reached New York and what it would be like to stay with my cousin Elizabeth, who I called Liz. She was a chef for a family on Long Island. I couldn't wait to see her.

She came to our house for Sunday dinner church at Pilgrim Rest at least once a month. Momma and Daddy paid her rent and loaned her money in Aberdeen. She was my momma's cousin from West Point, Mississippi, and she was about fifteen years older than me. Elizabeth was divorced with one son, Bobby (Boog) McMillian. She was a tall lady with freckles and a high-pitched voice who had left Aberdeen about five years earlier to find a job. When she packed her bags to leave Aberdeen and move to New York, she offered to send a ticket for me.

I had contacted my cousin after I left Tuskegee in 1964 because I needed a job. When I told her about my trip, she replied, "You're finally ready to leave Aberdeen," and told me that she would meet me at the Trailways bus station on Forty-Second Street when I arrived in the city.

When I got off the bus at the Port Authority, I looked around but didn't see Liz. Suddenly, there was a tap on my shoulder, and when I turned, my cousin embraced me. My new adventure had officially begun.

New York City, I am going to live here. I am standing in the city with eight million people! I staggered up the steps with Liz to Forty-Second Street and drew my first breath of the city. I felt like I had landed on Mars. I marveled at the noise of the car horns and watched the yellow cabs racing along the street. When I looked up at the tall skyscrapers, the super-tall structures sprouting in the sky, I wondered who lived in those expensive buildings. Probably movie stars like Sidney Poitier or Gregory Peck. I couldn't imagine living on the fortieth floor and having to walk up those steps to get home every day.

I was mesmerized, and it was like being on another planet, especially since I came from a small town with one stoplight. I noticed a thousand people walking on the streets, and they all seemed to be in a hurry to reach their destinations. Nobody stopped to say, "Hi, y'all." The sound of honking horns, blowing whistles, and cabs roaring down Fifth Avenue were all part of the enchanting environment. In Aberdeen, one car might pass every thirty minutes at a slow speed. On the corner of Forty-Second Street in New York, vendors hawked warm pretzels and juicy hot dogs and kebabs at a cheap price; this was eating on the go, and those mobile vendors were a unique part of New York City. I was thrilled, and I wanted a slice of that famous "New York-style" pizza.

I stretched my neck to gaze at the tall skyscrapers with their glass windows. Indeed, I wanted to shop at that big store, Macy's on Thirty-Fourth Street, to buy one of those Calvin Klein handbags. Ever since I was a little girl, Momma had told me to be courteous and wear stylish clothing. So now that I was in New York, I needed to fit into the city atmosphere. I was a country girl, but I wanted to adjust to the energy of New York City. In my mind, I still hear the song "New York, New York" by Frank Sinatra. This melody makes me think of the glitter and challenges of surviving in a city with eight million people.

At the corner of Forty-Second Street and Eighth Avenue, we went down the stairs to buy a token for twenty-five cents. The subway, which is in a tunnel, smelled strange to me. There were many different trains passing through the terminal to transfer to Yankee Stadium and Central Park. This seemed to be an enormous transportation station, and it was unlike anything I have ever seen. I went through the turnstile and onto the platform. As the train pulled into the station, I looked at the graffiti on the subway cars with its visual expression of art in yellow and blue, which I thought was interesting.

I carried my luggage onto the A train to Brooklyn, which was crowded with a variety of passengers that included a woman with her briefcase, a shirtless guy, and a blind man. I sat down on a linear metal seat with belts above to hang onto. The few riders sat next to each other and talked, but most were in their own world. The train car was clean inside with a bunch of advertisements for Broadway shows on the wall.

I marveled at white and Black people sitting together and smiling at each other. I asked my cousin, Liz, "Is this normal for the races to sit together?" I was surprised when she said yes! "Is there a colored section?" I asked. "No," Liz said with a smile. "No more Jim Crow Laws. You're in New York, not in Mississippi," she said, and we both chuckled.

Liz explained that I could go into restaurant through the front door without being arrested. I can't believe it. "But there is still racism in New York."

"Elizabeth," I said, "you know that we couldn't sit close to a white person in Aberdeen." Suddenly, I was discovering a new consciousness about my brown skin, and I still had so many questions. I wondered if I still needed to fear the police, among other things. Still, my spirit had been awakened to "the city that never sleeps."

"Elizabeth, I am going to like the Big Apple!"

While we rode the train, Elizabeth told me about a young man named Joseph. She told me that he was well-mannered and spent hours studying at the New York Public Library. *He is probably a nerd*, I thought. I wasn't excited about meeting him because I was just in New York to find a job for the summer.

Elizabeth had met Joseph's cousins, Ruth and James Irby, at the Bridge Street Baptist Church on Stuyvesant Street in Brooklyn through friends and began to visit them on her weekends. She uttered, "I met Joseph at a Sunday dinner, and she remembered that he was polite and chatted about jazz musicians like Miles Davis."

We exited the train and walked three blocks to her apartment at 348 Jefferson Avenue on the ninth floor. This was unlike my home in Aberdeen. Not only did this huge apartment building have many families and lots of barking dogs, but we walked up nine flights of stairs—no elevator, like many buildings in New York City. There were men hanging on the corner and kids riding their bikes.

I unpacked my suitcase, and Cousin Elizabeth introduced me to her neighbors. I met her friend Gloria in apartment 3A, who had a daughter around my age named Jasmine, and Edna and her husband in 4B. Gloria offered to take me to Coney Island, an amusement park. Elizabeth had organized a party for me with soul and reggae music so I could meet her friends. The side table had nachos with jalapeños. I saw a couple of people drinking Budweiser beer, and I had never seen my daddy drank a beer. I settled for iced tea.

I noticed a tall soldier who wore a green army uniform. He was sipping on a Coca-Cola at the table. Joseph came over to say hello in his deep voice. I was excited to meet him, but I pretended not to care. I was wearing my white jeans, a pink T-shirt, and silver sandals, and I said hello with my Southern accent; I was a little shy.

Joseph had thick eyebrows and glowing brown skin; he was rather good-looking in his green army uniform. He had a cast on his right leg from an accident at Fort Bragg army base, which gave us something to talk about at first. When I met other guys, I felt somewhat indifferent. But Joseph made me think about touching his hand. He seemed intelligent, and he was eager to learn about me.

Joseph talked to me about the borough of Brooklyn and the segregated neighborhood in the north-central portion commonly known as Bedford-Stuyvesant. It is the home of the great Jackie Robinson. There were small restaurants serving Caribbean and Southern food with rows of townhouses. He told me about the Jamaican restaurant on Nostrand Avenue near Jefferson Avenue that served jerk chicken, and gumbo which he mentioned was spicy. "Maybe I can take you there for lunch," he suggested, and I told him I'd think about it.

We chatted about Coney Island, and he had been there swimming. I told him I couldn't wait to walk on the sand. Joseph continued to talk about his visits to see Ruth and James and how his dad used to hang out with Cousin James in their younger days.

"I was born at Harlem Hospital," Joseph told me, and "I lived with my parents in Washington Heights until I enlisted into the army." I soon learned that he had been in the army for three months. Until he'd enlisted in the army, he had worked for his dad, who managed a four-story apartment building on 155th Street. Finally, Joseph mentioned that he liked the New York Knicks basketball team, and he was good at shooting hoops with his cousins.

Next, he asked me about Aberdeen. I told him, "It's a small town, and I sit on the front porch to holler at our neighbors. I suppose there are about five thousand folks; my family consists of my mom, Estell, my dad, Wardell, and my sister. We live in this white house on Matubba Street with my dog, Spooky, who has gray fur. Sometimes, he sneaks him into my room to sleep under the bed. I make sure he doesn't bark, otherwise, Momma would start yelling, 'Why is Spooky in my house.' And I plan to return to Tuskegee in the fall."

Joseph listened carefully to everything I told him, and when I finished, he remarked, "I see that you are ready to achieve your goals. Your cousin Elizabeth told me about you. As I said, I had some challenges with segregation in Aberdeen. I decided to leave my small town and to work in a big city.

Joseph soon asked me to dance, and my heart was pounding. He held my hand while we dance to "Baby Love" by the Supremes. At the end of the party, we exchanged phone numbers. I would have called him first, but I did not want to seem pushy.

About a month later, Joseph and I went on a date. He took me to see a Broadway show on Forty-Fifth Street. I got all dressed up to see *Hello, Dolly!* with Carol Channing and Louis Armstrong. That night on stage, I saw movie stars for the first time in my life. Joseph had good manners, and he was polite.

∽

About three weeks later, I went to the Apollo Theater for the first time. It was amateur night, and I was with my cousin, Liz, and Gloria's daughter Jasmine, who was tall with brown skin, long, curly hair to her shoulders and a body like Twiggy, the super-skinny model. When I saw the huge billboard with its blinking lights, I just wanted to stand there and admire the image. I had read about the history of the famous Apollo, which had opened in 1934. (After that evening, I called my sister, Mary, to let her know I'd visited a place I had dreamed about for years.)

The line at the theater snaked around the building. It seemed everyone from the neighborhood was there. Of course, I had my Kodak Instamatic camera, just to capture the moment. On the way to my seat in the lower level in the middle section, I passed a display of celebrity photos on the wall, entertainers like Red Foxx and Ray Charles; when I thought about Aretha Franklin and James Brown, who performed on the Apollo's stage ... I supposed there were many stories in those hallowed halls.

I don't recall the show's host that night, but he was funny. As each act appeared, I screamed and yelled with Jasmine. If a performer was awful, Sandman Sims in the ugly hat yanked them off the stage while the audience hollered, "Get off the stage!"

Even before the Apollo, there was the Savoy Ballroom on Lenox Avenue in Harlem, known as "The World's Finest Ballroom" and "Home of Happy Feet." It was a place where musicians and dancers could showcase their talents. For many years, Black performers had to enter through the back door at theaters and clubs to perform and earn an income. These performers still lack the respect that they deserve today. Still, the Apollo continued the tradition of displaying Black performers with jazz singers like Ella Fitzgerald and Sarah Vaughan. As a Southern girl, I'd always wanted to sit in the audience at the Apollo and feel the love from the audience. And I just knew that New York is the place where I wanted to be!

9

Joseph

JOSEPH AND I began spending more time together, and one warm Sunday afternoon in October, I met his parents in the Bronx. They greeted me with a warm embrace. His dad, who was also named Joseph, was a decorated World War II veteran with muscles like a weightlifter. He worked as a maintenance man for a four-story building in Harlem. Joseph's mom, Carrie, was Catholic. She had long, thick, gray hair, and the day I met them, we sat in the living room on a leather sofa, and she served a chocolate espresso layer cake. Joseph's dad, who was short with a balding head, said, "I am happy to meet a girl from the South who likes my son. How do you like this fast pace in New York?" I told him I was adjusting to walking down Forty-Second Street and finding the Seventh Avenue subway station.

Soon, there was a knock on the door, and a bunch of Joseph's family members sauntered into the room. I began to get nervous because Joseph hadn't told me that I was meeting his whole family. There was his younger brother Anthony, who was twelve years old and wore a Yankee's baseball cap, his brother Herbie, who was three years younger than Joseph, and his cousin Eugene, who wore a leather jacket. His Aunt Frankie, his dad's sister, and his cousin Michael, who was tall like Joseph, piled into the apartment too. Later, I met Joseph's grandmother, Sadie Halliburton, from South Carolina.

The spotlight was on me, and I was nervous with the family evaluating me, yet I was confident in my gray miniskirt, black suede boots, and thick orange sweater. I told them about growing up in Aberdeen and about my sister, Mary, who allowed me to wear her clothes to church on Sunday. Aunt Frankie remarked, "I see that you got my nephew excited about you. Well, I don't ever remember him introducing us to a girlfriend." His cousins chimed in eagerly, saying that Joseph had been doing a lot of smiling lately. In the meantime, Joseph sat next to me on the loveseat, wearing his military uniform. Cousin Michael told stories about them playing stickball in the streets of Harlem. Before the family left for home, I got plenty of hugs. I told Joseph when they were gone, "Your family reminds me of my cousins in Aberdeen with their witty stories about you."

I was still sitting on the loveseat with Joseph when this big, tall bloodhound dog named Teddy came to stand near him. I think my heart skipped a beat because he was a huge dog, a hound with a smooth red coat who stood two feet tall and weighed about 100 pounds. Panting, he came to stand by my chair, and Joseph said, "I think he likes you." I wasn't so sure … I mean … I didn't really feel the love, so Joseph led Teddy to the kitchen for a treat. Months later, when I stayed with the family, Teddy sat on his bottom and leaned toward my plate, so I fed him several pieces of my Jiffy cornbread. I was so relieved that he liked me!

ᑲ

When I first arrived in New York, I stayed with Elizabeth in her small apartment on Tompkins Avenue in Brooklyn for a month. Soon, Joseph's cousin James and his wife, Ruth, offered me their spare bedroom. I couldn't believe they refused to accept any money, and they told me I could live with them until I got my own place. Ruth, who was around fifty years old, got on my nerves sometimes, seeing that she checked on me when I went out with Joseph or my girlfriend Jasmine. She would often ask, "What time are you coming home?" It was annoying, but I assumed she was just trying to protect me. Anyway, she decorated my room with aqua and white curtains and a matching bedspread, and she took my clothes to the laundry every week. Ruth and her husband both worked on Flatbush Avenue in Brooklyn at a Sears warehouse. Ruth was an usher at her church, and I often went to church with them on Sunday mornings. We'd stop for breakfast at the diner on the corner before church. I rode with them in their fancy 1965 Fleetwood Cadillac while James smoked his smelly cigar.

༄

My mission was to return to Tuskegee. I remembered that I had wanted to pursue my passion for learning in college and changing my life from the time I had been on the plantation. I wanted to make my family proud of me because I had witnessed their struggles to survive and of being marginalized. When I met Joseph in New York at nineteen years old, I was no longer certain about my plan for college. I was falling in love with Joseph. The urban lifestyle with Joseph had me animated and full of vitality, yet I was worried about my future. One thing I knew for sure was that I would finish college because that was my dream. I prayed that my decision to stay in New York was the right one.

༄

In September, two months after we met, Joseph told me that he wanted me to be his wife. Around that same time, I wrote a letter to my sister about meeting him.

Hi Mary,

Cousin Liz introduced me to Joseph when I got to Brooklyn. I am staying in New York City, and I put my return to Tuskegee on hold for now. You won't believe it, girl, but I was smitten with this guy when I first met him. He is handsome with a silver tongue. With his deep voice, he tells me stories about the Apollo Theatre and about his family from South Carolina. This guy is in the army, and he is six feet tall with thick eyebrows and light brown skin. When I look into those big brown eyes, I could listen to him talk all day. He sings "Moody's Mood for Love" by jazz musician James Moody. When he is holding my hand, I feel like a queen. Not to mention I fall asleep at night dreaming about his songs. Girl, something has changed about me. Joseph has rocked my world. It's magic between us. One thing for sure, I won't be coming back to Aberdeen. I am in New York to grow and to live a life that makes me happy. And I am making intentional choices. I know that Momma warned me about the slick guys in New York. Since I am a country girl from the South and he is a Northerner, is Joseph really the guy for me?

I told Daddy about Joseph, and he said, "Sis, come home. You're too young to be in that big city."

Now that I am staying in New York, I really enjoy walking the trails with Joseph at Central Park in the middle of New York City. It has sprawling flower gardens, and it's the largest park that I have seen in my life. Mary, I miss you and my dog Spooky. Love you, always.

⌒◯

I knew that Joseph was a soldier, but I never thought I would be serious about him. I just liked walking down Fifth Avenue in New York and standing in front of a store window and seeing our shadow.

I enjoyed hanging out with this tall soldier in New York City, with its collection of towering skyscrapers and herds of people marching along the street in a hurry. It seems like I am in a movie. It does not seem real that I am finding my purpose in New York. Plus, Joseph is witty and always singing jazz songs, like "God Bless the Child" by Billy Holliday. When we stopped in a deli near Central Park and shared a cream cheese bagel with an iced coffee, it was like we were the only ones in the room. After dating Joseph for three months, I realized that I looked forward to seeing him, and I found myself waiting for his phone calls. Then he began calling me his wife when he'd introduce me to other people. I just considered him being foolish, and I thought that he was a little crazy.

Today, I would tell my younger self that I was foolish not to return to Tuskegee and finish my education. I could have gone to the City College of New York, but at the time, I thought my choices were limited. Indeed, I was fearful in the city when I arrived, but I found a family that cared for me. My decision to marry Joseph was the right one. How many times in this world do you find someone you can trust? It was my time to set my own path and to value my own opinion as a Black woman. I am grateful for my journey!

⌒

I found a part-time job at a small dress shop on Nostrand Avenue in Brooklyn, but Jasmine had a friend who worked at Gimbels department store in Manhattan near Thirty-Fourth Street. It was a job for a clerk. Well, one cold October morning we climbed on the Lexington train into Manhattan. Jasmine had seen an ad in the *New York Post* for a retail clerk and cashier; it paid $1.25 an hour, and she told me, "That's more than what I am making at J. C. Penney." I was excited about getting a new job, so I spent hours choosing the right outfit for this job interview, and I finally decided on a gold shift dress that was just above the knee, with a small matching purse. Jasmine wore a green pencil dress with a white collar. Then we decided to wear our black leather heels. I told Jasmine to tone it down and not to wear long eyelashes.

As we sauntered into Gimbels with its fancy, shiny door and passed through the aisles filled with pillbox hats and designer handbags, I had to drag Jasmine away from the makeup counter, reminding her, "We are here for a job, remember?"

I stepped on the elevator with Jasmine beside me and pushed the bottom to the second floor where the employment office was located. After I signed the sheet at the front desk, I told the receptionist that I wanted to apply for the clerk's job. She told me to wait for the manager.

I began telling Jasmine about Joseph surprising me with a gold necklace for dinner after he left the base at Governors Island in New York. Jasmine shared that she wanted to see *Porgy and Bess* on Broadway, but her boyfriend had canceled their date. After we'd waited for an hour and were the only ones in the waiting room, I asked my friend, "Jasmine, are you sure that they hire Colored in this store?" "Yes," she answered, "I saw a brown-skinned saleslady with a name tag. I assumed that she worked in the lingerie department." I thought about that for a moment, and then I told her, "You see, girl, in Aberdeen, there was no chance that I could ever work in a department store. If you did work there, it was behind a mop or a broom." Jasmine got up, went to the window, and knocked on the sliding screen. We could hear the phone ringing, but no one answered her knocks.

After we'd been waiting for two hours, I marched to the window and banged on the counter. The receptionist answered, "I didn't know that you folks were still waiting," she said.

I stood with my purse on the counter and told her we were waiting for our interviews. "I told you the manager is occupied," the woman responded. She talked with tight lips like she was angry.

We continued to sit and wait, anxiously looking at the clock on the wall. Two young white ladies signed in at the desk. About ten minutes later, they were called back to the office with a smile. By then, we had been waiting for three hours.

Finally, Jasmine was called back for her interview with the manager, which lasted for ten minutes. Next, the manager called "Estell Halibut," which annoyed me. I was led into a small room with a folding chair and a metal table with a rotating fan in the ceiling. I handed the manager my application. Karen, the manager who wore red lipstick and a black suit, glanced at my application and then tucked back her brunette hair. As she looked over the long sheet, she asked, "I see that you are from Mississippi. Are you married?" No, I told her. "Do you have any children?" No, again. Karen fiddled with her eyebrows. "That job for a retail clerk is no longer open," she announced. And I believe that she threw my application in the wastepaper basket. I stared at Karen for a moment before I stomped out of her office.

My heart was racing with anger. I clutched my purse and shouted, "Jasmine, let's go." Sweat dripped from my forehead, and I wanted to shake that lady. "You know, Estell," Jasmine told me as we marched through the store on our way out, "she asked me about my religion. And her second question was 'did I ever get fired from a job?'" I was upset, so I don't remember leaving the office, but I recall gritting my teeth. I told Jasmine, "This will not stop me from getting another job."

We quickly exited the building and scooted across Thirty-Fifth Street to the vendor on the corner to get one of those warm Nathan's hot dogs with extra sauce. "Jasmine," I told my friend sadly, "I am learning that New York with its tall skyscrapers is still like the South in many ways."

⌒⊙

In October, Joseph took me on the shuttle to Governors Island, where he was a medic on the army base. We took a cab to lower Manhattan and rode the Staten Island Ferry, and I could see the Statue of Liberty, the towering figure with a torch in her right hand and clutching a tablet in her left. I was mesmerized just looking at it. The boat passed the Brooklyn skyline, which has a vast coastline with rocky edges. When I got on the ferry, it was moving slightly, and Joseph held my hand while the wind blew my curls. I wore a pink scarf around my neck and a blue turtleneck sweater on the crowded boat. This was my first time on a boat, and it was an awesome adventure. Joseph asked another passenger who was from Long Island, New York, to snap our picture with the Statue of Liberty in the background.

When we got on the base, we stopped at the military base station to check in. I showed my ID, and then we walked about two blocks to the small hospital that treated patients. I met Sergeant Oliver, who was in charge. Joseph introduced me as his wife. I don't remember a lot about the place other than it smelled like disinfectant and had sparkling white walls, and around each corner were military men in uniforms.

While I was at the base, I met Jocelyn, who worked at the PX, and I learned that her husband had just left for Vietnam. She had seen me with Joseph and said, "You look happy, is that your boyfriend?" "Yes," I told her, "I met him a few months ago." Then Jocelyn told me, "You know that he might be heading to Vietnam." Joseph had not mentioned going to Vietnam. When I finished shopping, I asked Jocelyn for her phone number because she reminded me of my best friend in high school with her smile.

When Joseph left for Fort Bragg, North Carolina, in November 1964, he wanted me to go with him as his girlfriend, and I could stay on the base. I told him no, and that he could talk to me when he was ready to put a ring on my finger. Anyway, I wasn't ready to get married.

I wanted to be with Joseph, but my home in New York with my friends and Cousin Liz was stable. I had a job and my own money. Although I was unhappy when I wasn't with my boyfriend, when I stepped out onto the streets of Manhattan, I found New York to be inviting. There was something so alluring about living in the city. Joseph was displeased about my decision and a little peeved for a while. But I believe he understood my feelings, especially knowing that I came from a small town with limited access to a decent job. New York had been a big dream of mine in high school, and this was the beginning of my success story. I told Joseph that I liked him, but I wanted to be independent. Being on my own at twenty years old was a little scary, and it seemed that the red dirt from the cotton field was still on my heels. However, Joseph made me feel that I could accomplish my dreams.

While he was at Fort Bragg, I worked and spent my spare time riding the subway to shop at boutiques near Fifth Avenue. During the holiday in November, I hopped on the train with Jasmine for our trip to join the crowd on Thirty-Fourth Street to watch the Macy's Thanksgiving Day Parade. I saw Mickey Mouse balloons floating in the air while I was squeezed and surrounded by a dense group of people from the Midwest. But no matter what else was going on, the parade was amazing! For many years I had viewed the parade on TV on Thanksgiving in Aberdeen. Jasmine wore a sweater to show off her curves, but I wore my boots with a red hooded jacket, telling her, "I am not freezing in twenty-degree weather."

⌒

Joseph came home on leave from Fort Bragg, the army base in North Carolina, for three weeks before leaving for Vietnam. He stayed with his parents in the Bronx. I did not know he was home.

It was January 1965. I was curled up on my bed with the car horns and firetrucks on Jefferson Avenue howling through the street in the background. Since I had been in New York, I'd adapted to the sounds and the city's neon lights. That day, I was just turning the pages of *Jet* magazine when Ruth pushed the door ajar. "Estell, I think there is someone to see you," she said. *Oh really, someone to see me?* I thought. I took the rollers out of my hair and strolled into the living room in my blue jeans and a lavender crew-neck cardigan. I gazed around the empty room with its tall ceiling and dim lights, wondering what was going on. Suddenly, here comes Joseph in a blue suit and tie, shined leather shoes, a neat haircut, and a huge smile on his face. Keeping his eyes on me, he got down on one knee and handed me a yellow rose. I sat on the brown sofa, and he gripped my hand tightly.

"Estell," Joseph said, "I want you to be my wife. Will you marry me?"

My face lit up like a flashlight, and I hesitated for a moment, bubbling with excitement. I took a deep breath and said, "Yes, I will marry you."

Joseph took my left hand and slipped a diamond ring on my third finger. He said, "When I danced with you on Jefferson Avenue in July, I knew that you were for me!" and he wrapped his arms around me.

The rush of excitement just boiled over, and I hollered, "I am engaged!" Then we sat on the couch, Joseph holding me close, and he kissed me; it was pure magic.

Joseph looked into my eyes and said, "You brought sunshine into my life, and I love your Southern manner."

"You know, Joseph, I knew that you were special when I heard you call my name. By the way, you look different out of your army uniform," I said, and he chuckled.

"My mom told me that I needed to look my best tonight," he confessed.

Soon, Ruth and James marched into the living room with a bottle of champagne. "Congratulations!" they said as they embraced us, and then I drank my first glass of sparkling pink champagne to celebrate. James teased his cousin, "Joseph, I told you that you were going to marry that Mississippi girl." Ruth put a 45-rpm record to spin on the portable Victrola. "My Girl" by the Temptations played while we danced like we were in the moonlight. *I can't believe that I am actually engaged to the man I love*, I thought, and I felt like I was on another planet. I kept wondering what my mom and dad were going to say. But I loved Joseph, and that was an awesome night. Joseph whispered into my ear, "You are awesome!" I was engaged to the man I loved, and I had to keep reminding myself that this was real. I did not want to let go of his hand when he finally left for home after midnight.

As soon as he was gone, I called Mary in Aberdeen. "Sis, are you all right? It's after midnight," she said, her voice filled with worry.

"Yes. Joseph asked me to marry him, and I said yes! Mary, I was swept off my feet!"

"Sis, I am so happy for you. When can I meet Joseph?"

"It will be a while before he comes to Aberdeen," I told her. "He had never eaten at a lunch counter where they refuse to serve you because of the color of your skin. I'm not sure that he's ready to drink from a separate water fountain."

"Did you ever tell Joseph the true story about growing up in Aberdeen and picking cotton on the plantation?" Mary asked.

"I will tell him," I assured her, "but it is painful to talk about."

In a loving voice, she babbled, "I am so happy for you, Sis."

∽

Joseph received his orders for Vietnam in January 1965. Just two days later, he was at the city clerk's office purchasing a marriage license for two dollars; he had proposed to me as soon as he got his orders. His Uncle Jalen from Harlem helped Joseph purchase our wedding rings from Katz Jewelry store on Forty-Seventh Street, and we were married two weeks later.

On January 23, 1965, I became Mrs. Joseph Halliburton. The ceremony was quickly arranged by his mom, Carrie. I was nervous before the ceremony. I wore my white suit and stacked heels, and Joseph wore his green army uniform when we tied the knot.

We were married at the two-story brownstone residence at 140th Street and Seventh Avenue in Harlem, at a brownstone of Carrie's friend Evelyn on a cold Saturday afternoon with snow piling up on the sidewalk. I recalled saying our vows, and his mom, with tears in her eyes, saying, "Welcome to the family, daughter." Joseph carried me over the threshold, and the family threw rice at us. The tradition of being carried over the threshold was a form of "jumping the broom," which reclaims a tradition that was started in slavery and was made famous in the movie *Roots*. It symbolizes a new beginning—the joining of two families and letting go of the past.

After the ceremony, I remember thinking, *Girl, you are just nineteen years old, what are you doing?* And then I thought, *I'm in love with this handsome army soldier!*

When I called my parents to share the news, my dad was quite troubled about me marrying a guy from New York who was in the army. "Sis," he asked, "do you know anything about his upbringing?" When I told Joseph about my dad's concern, Joseph said, "Your dad was all fired up about our marriage. I will prove to him that I deserve you." My momma's response was, "Sis, I love you, you are my baby." I hadn't heard those words from Momma in years. I knew she loved me, but we had our differences. Now she supported me, and Daddy was just worried about my marriage. I knew they would always be there for me. My dad wanted me to come home to Aberdeen because he believed that New York was no place for a young girl, but I stayed with Joseph's parents while he was overseas.

Joseph was ready to be a soldier and serve his country like his dad. When he left for Vietnam in February of 1965, we had only been together for six months, and I moped around for a week. Soon though, I got up every morning, prepared my breakfast, and walked to the subway with a smile for my job in Manhattan.

10

Life as a Newlywed

B EFORE JOSEPH LEFT New York for Vietnam on Tuesday,
February 2, 1965, we lived with his parents, Carrie and Joseph,
on Popular Street in the Bronx. We were newlyweds, married
for just ten days, when he left for Vietnam.

Carrie knew how alone I felt once Joseph was gone. One morning,
she surprised me after breakfast. "Daughter, come check out this box
under the table." I strolled into the kitchen and saw a blue basket
with a red bow. I opened it, and inside was an adorable brown-and-
white beagle puppy with little droopy brown ears, a square face, and
a white-and-brown tail. What an adorable face!

"How old is my puppy?" I asked Carrie, who responded that
the beagle was two months old. "The neighbors down the street had
two puppies," she explained, "and they were looking for a home
for them. I decided that I would surprise you! I knew this would
make you smile."

I cradled my puppy in my arms and laid him on my shoulder. I
asked her if I would have to pick up poop behind him, and she told
me yes, that was the law in New York.

I decided to name him "Buddy" while he was snuggling near my neck. He became my best friend while Joseph was in Vietnam. In Aberdeen, my dog slept on the porch and played in the yard, but as Buddy grew older, he crawled up on the couch, laid his head in my lap, and watched *Gunsmoke* with me. Buddy liked playing with tennis balls; he knocked over my pink lamp while running in the living room more than once. I scolded him a bit, but Buddy showed me so much love!

◦⃝

Before Joseph's departure, Carrie helped me decorate the living room with red roses for our candlelight dinner. I wore the pink sweater he'd bought for me for Christmas.

I spent hours in the kitchen putting together my special dinner of spaghetti and meat sauce with mushroom and hot peppers. I did my best to remember my momma's recipe for the sauce. Joseph cleaned his plate, so I guess it was all right! We sat on the blue love seat, and he wore his white T-shirt and slacks. Joseph took off his dog tags and put them around my neck. He just looked into my eyes and said, "I love you, and I am so blessed that we are married. I will never forget you, Estell." I remember a tear rolled down my cheek as we sat there together, his arm around my shoulder. I thought about my brother Alfred, who was killed in Korea, his life cut short at twenty-three years old, and how they identified him by his dog tags. Joseph was going to Vietnam as an ammunition technician. His job would be dismantling bombs in his squad. Would I ever see him again?

We used our moments together that evening to reminisce about our picnic lunches in Central Park. I fixed tortilla chips with salsa, lemon pepper wings, and iced tea to settle down on our blanket. The wall clock ticked while our time inched away.

Joseph left the room to shave, and the smell of his Old Spice permeated the apartment. As we counted down the minutes we had left together, Nina Simone sang "Sugar in My Bowl" on the small record player.

I helped Joseph pack his duffel bag, and he insisted that I pack our wedding pictures. As we slowly headed to the door with locked hands, Joseph's dad was waiting. He placed his hand on Joseph's shoulder and gripped it, saying, "You make me proud, fighting to protect our country." Carrie stood next to him, her eyes filled with tears, and told her son, "I am praying that you come home safely." Joseph, his jaw tight, responded, "I will, Mom." Suddenly, he lifted me off the floor, hugged me, and said, "I will miss you, babe!"

I looked into his big brown eyes for what I feared could be the last time. Joseph made me feel like we were bonded together forever. Then, he squeezed my hand with my wedding ring, saying, "So long." I sobbed as he went out the door. Wearing his green army fatigues and carrying his duffel bag, he went down the stairs and turned to wave one last time. Then, he left for La Guardia Airport in New York to connect with his unit in North Carolina and on to Vietnam.

The door closed, leaving Carrie and me alone in the room. I plopped down in the chair and just began wringing my hands. Carrie said, "Daughter, you gonna be fine." She rubbed my shoulder and then guided me to my bedroom. When I passed the photograph of my husband, PFC Joseph R. Halliburton, on the night table, a feeling of loss flowed over my body, and a wailing cry and weeping came over me. Carrie sat on the bed beside me until I fell asleep.

After breakfast, my dad called from Aberdeen, asking if I was all right. He asked if I wanted to come home for a while since Joseph was deployed to Vietnam. I told him no. But I felt a source of strength in his kind words. I knew from listening to my dad that it was my time to be independent.

It would be weeks before I would hear from my husband. I realized that I couldn't control everything in my life. I believed God would show me the way. However, I could make my own decision to continue my journey as an army wife. I decided to call Jocelyn, who I'd met at Governor's Island, and explain to her that Joseph had left for Vietnam. I would tell her, "I don't like this waiting for him and not knowing when I will get a letter from him. Already, I miss him so much, and he will be gone for thirteen months."

When Jocelyn answered the phone, I recognized her squeaky voice. "My husband just left for Vietnam," I told her. Jocelyn's words rang in my ears, "Sister Estell, I am here for you. Our husbands are fighting for our country in Vietnam, and you and I are married to warriors. It's our duty to take care of the home front while they are gone." She suggested I call a group called Military Wives, which could offer support. I did contact the group, and I met Kristen, who called every week to check on me.

∽

Joseph stayed in Vietnam for thirteen months. On Saturday nights, I lay on the sofa watching James Bond movies and wondering what was happening in the war. I dreaded watching the evening news or seeing pictures of soldiers with helmets in the jungle and piles of dead bodies being shipped back to America. *Is he in the jungle or the rice field with his unit? I am sure he is protecting our country, and I know that he cares for me* were some of the thoughts I had. Joseph's family kept me occupied; his mom would sometimes bring me potted green Hibiscus plants or a pastrami sandwich from the Jewish deli.

I mailed a letter to Joseph every week. Once, I sent him a greeting card that opened with wide-stretched arms to give him a hug. Of course, I put Chanel No. 5 perfume on the envelope.

It took a month or sometimes six weeks before he received his mail because he was in the jungle fighting with his Saigon-based unit. I often packed up sardines, Spaghetti O's, peppermint candy, peanut butter and crackers, and dried fruits and shipped them to him.

While Joseph was gone, I was on a strict budget because I received only $49.00 a month as military spouse.

I needed a job, and I needed to upgrade my skills to get a job, so I enrolled in a six-week accounting class. Afterward, I got a job at Guerlain, the company that sold Shalimar perfume. It was located on Thirty-Third Street and a block from the Empire State Building, the tallest building in the city at that time. Guerlain was on the fifth floor, and the offices had thick maroon carpet and bright colored walls. I wore a blue dress and beige leather heels or the interview. I was interviewed by Miss Godwin, the supervisor, who had brown hair and wore a well-tailored white suit. After my forty-minute interview, she asked when I could start. I stammered, "I … I can start on Monday!"

When I walked into the office that first day, it was silent … my new coworkers just stared until I sat down at my desk. I guess they thought I was from outer space. Ashly, a skinny white lady who was the manager, came over to my desk and explained my duties. I worked in a cubicle near the back, and I quickly acquired the knowledge to operate the adding and copying machines. The women did not talk to me at the office, and the manager just put work sheets on my desk. During the coffee break, I sat alone. There was my world at home and the one inside the office, where I was ignored.

One day at work, I heard the team up front talking about Muhammad Ali, the boxer, and Ashly said, "These people need to go back to Africa where they belong." I was shocked to hear those words in New York, and I realized this city had bigots, too. Finally, Susan, one of my coworkers, came to share coffee with me. Still, I was not part of the team on the job. I worked there for six months. And I saw this as another experience where my coworkers only saw the color of my skin.

Still, I had a sense of freedom in NYC that I never had in Mississippi—people could speak up and do what they wanted to do.

There were so many rules in the South we had to follow to stay alive, and we had to speak and act a certain way. Prejudice in the North was quiet and mostly unspoken.

My next-door neighbor Deanna, who was from Mobile, Alabama, often came with me when I went shopping. She had been in Brooklyn for five years. "You know, Estell," she told me one day, "my mom asked me to come back home to Mobile. Girl, I won't be riding on the back of the bus. No, I ain't never going back. The Black folk know their rights in New York.'" I struggled with that too; as I told Deanna, there was bigotry in Aberdeen, yet I looked forward to seeing my mom and dad that summer. "Since I have been in New York," I told her, "I am learning to value my thoughts and feel grateful each day."

When Joseph left for Vietnam, I was lonely. I went to Chock full o'Nuts near Fifty-Ninth Street where we use to hang out and ordered hot chocolate, but it just wasn't the same. When I returned to my apartment, Buddy, my puppy with the cute ears, always greeted me at the front door, and it was so comforting to rub his thick fur.

I had settled into a routine of going to work and coming home to write in my journal, but I was looking for something more to occupy my time. On a Monday afternoon in February 1965, when my husband had been gone for thirty days, my phone rang. It was my friend Jacqueline, who said, "I got good news for you. Can I stop by for a visit?"

I met Jacqueline on Jefferson Avenue when I first arrived in New York. She offered to show me around the city, and she was a model. She often came to my home and told me details about her modeling career, and I was intrigued.

The doorbell rang, and I opened the door to the scent of Dior perfume. Standing there and holding a bright red box of candy for me was Jacqueline, who had a professional look of success. With her tall, slender frame and high cheekbones, she was stunning. Just the right amount of makeup enhanced her coffee-brown skin, and her long curls rested on her shoulders. She wore knee-length suede boots and held a maroon designer handbag. "Hello, Estell," she greeted me, and then leaned in for a hug.

After I invited her inside, we sat on the gray couch. I couldn't help but notice a blue sapphire ring on her middle finger as we chatted. I kept imagining that fancy ring in my jewelry box.

"I came over to offer you a part-time job as a model," Jacqueline said.

"I already have a job," I replied. "I am working in an office and getting a good salary." And I tried to imagine myself as a model. Modeling seemed frightening, and I would need to learn all these things, like how to speak and pose. I am not ready to have someone judge my looks or how I walk "I am not sure that I am ready to work as a model," I told her.

Jacqueline smiled and then said, "This is your opportunity to be independent. It's hard work, but I know that you can do it. You've got the smile—and long legs."

I thought about that for a moment. I looked again at that dazzling ring on her finger and thought, *I like fine jewelry, and she must have a big bank account, too.* "All right," I told my friend, "You convinced me. When do I start?"

Jacqueline looked delighted. "I know that you'll like seeing your image on camera, and you like wearing different outfits. My agent is willing to help you get started," she continued. "I showed her a head-shot of you. Her name is Madeleine Klein, and she is the manager of the EL Modeling agency."

"Did you tell her that I have brown skin and thick hips?"

"Yeah, girl. She will be interviewing you on Friday."

"You mean I need to take off from work?"

"Yes." Jacqueline's tone became serious. "I have a checklist for you: makeup bag, moisturizer, hair spray, shoes. I'll help you, and I found someone to make you a portfolio. Guess what, Estell. You can earn twenty dollars an hour."

I was surprised! "Are you serious?" I added that I was making about a dollar thirty-five an hour on my job at Gilbert Carrier.

Jacqueline looked me over and said, "You might want to be a size six."

"I am a size eight," I confessed, "so I'll just be drinking water and eating carrot sticks," and we both laughed.

"Listen, Estell, you've got flawless brown skin, and you are ready," she assured me. I was nervous but excited about trying something new.

Soon after, Jacqueline left my apartment with a firm handshake that I would follow up with my appointment.

I kept in touch with Jacqueline, who later moved to California to earn more money. I will always remember how she believed in my talent to be a model.

☙

That Friday, I met Madeline, a short lady with gray hair, on Forty-First Street and Fifth Avenue. She invited me to "tell me about yourself," and I did.

"I like the tone of your voice," she responded, "and I need you to walk down the red carpet." After I did, she told me, "Jacqueline was right. I think you *are* good. I am sending you to a new fashion designer for leisure wear and catalog work."

Then, I went to a small office on Fifty-Ninth Street with my makeup bags. After I registered at the front desk, Madeleine's photographer, Matt, a young white guy with a ponytail, took about twenty photos. I kept thinking, *I have no idea what I am doing.*

I needed to make a good impression, so I kept about twelve photos that showed a variety of styles to create my modeling portfolio. That morning, I wore a sleeveless, lime-green fitted shirt, blue jeans, and slim, beige calf-length boots. Matt had me pose several ways: with my hands on my hips, looking over my shoulder, and sitting on a stool.

When Matt finished the photo shoot, which included a headshot, he said, "Estell, I enjoyed working with you. You have a great smile."

The next week, I stood in line for the catalog audition with twenty girls who had European features, thin lips, narrow noses, and straight hair. I was the only person there with brown skin other than a young Asian woman. While I was in line, I met Ella Mae from Huntsville, Alabama, who had a Southern accent. She had red hair and freckles; she was six feet tall with long legs. I introduced myself and told her I came from Mississippi. Ella Mae told me she had been a beauty queen, and she came to New York to be a model. I told her I was beginning a new career, too. Ella Mae squeezed my hand, and I was thinking, *I don't even know her.* But I was happy to have someone to chat with while we waited, though in the end, neither of us was chosen.

Madeline told me about a fashion show for charity that would be in Brooklyn and that they were seeking models to volunteer for a photoshoot. I knew I would benefit from the experience, so I decided to go. Just the thought of being in the show made me nervous; my brain kept thinking about everything that could go wrong, like tripping on the short runway while turning and my feet wobbling in my heels. Also, the lighting for camera shoots made me look shiny and pale, and there was no makeup for my dark skin.

Before my first show, I stayed awake all night thinking about it. When I stepped out the door onto the runway, the guy had to push me out on stage. I felt a little better when I heard loud clapping from the audience. The designer chose me to model leisure wear for the Spiegel catalog, and I did it. I loved modeling, and I was hooked.

During this time, I kept thinking about when I was fourteen years old, and my mother had me walk around with a book on my head for my posture. I thought that stuff was crazy back then. But here I was with my mother's voice in my head telling me, "Walk gracefully."

Later, I told Carrie about it, and she asked, "How do you think Joseph will feel about your modeling career?

Estell modeling at age 22. In 1967, I had short, curled hair and arched eyebrows, and lightly tinted makeup with pink lipstick. I was modeling in New York and feeling that I was not only beautiful, but I knew how to get around in the city and shop at Saks Fifth Avenue. I had become a part of the culture and enjoyed going to Broadway shows. Afterward, I sometimes dined at Momma Leones on West 44th Street, and other times, I walked the streets of Harlem. I enjoyed wearing designer clothes and having my own bank account while Joseph was in Vietnam.

"Well, I'll wait and see," was my response.

At the El Modeling agency, I met Nancy, who was twenty years old like me and wanted to be a model; we became good friends. Her mother was Black, and her father was white. Nancy, who had long reddish hair and lightly tinted skin, was outspoken. "I came to New York to get away from being called n****er," she told me.

I told her, "Girl, let me tell you that when I grew up in Aberdeen, I got tired of seeing the 'Colored Only' signs posted in town to remind me that was I was different and unworthy of walking through the front door of a restaurant."

꩜

Nancy and I soon learned that bigotry existed at the modeling agencies, too. One day, Nancy and I had an appointment at the Best Talent Agency for a print ad. "Do you think they are hiring Black models?" I asked Nancy. "Let's go and check it out!" With our portfolios and gray makeup bags in hand, we hailed a cab to Fifty-Fourth Street and Seventh Avenue, and once we arrived at the building, we walked up two flights of stairs. The secretary at the front desk told us, "The lounge for cleaning ladies is downstairs."

I said, "No! We are here from El Modeling agency." The woman's lips tightened. After the secretary made a phone call, she said coldly, "Miss Jones will see you now." She pointed to a blue door.

We entered a square room filled with the scent of hair spray and perfume. I was told by an attendant to change into new outfits with ten other models who were white. I removed my jacket, opened my tote bag, and sat down to wait with Nancy. When Miss Jones, the manager, saw us, she shouted, "We don't hire Black models. Our client only wants white models."

"Madeleine, our agent, sent us," Nancy told her.

"She knows that I hire only skinny models," the manager said.

The other models continued to talk like we weren't there. I stared at Miss Jones with my jaw clenched for a moment, and then I grabbed my shoes and purse and yelled, "Let's go!" Nancy's fists were balled up, and she was cursing. I pushed Nancy toward the door, and we left the office with my black leather high heels hitting the steps and Nancy trailing behind me.

As we stepped onto the street, Nancy said angrily, "That woman was cruel and hateful."

I said, "I am feeling bad that you did not get a chance to smack her. That was just another ignorant person."

⌒

Modeling was intimidating at first, and I thought my nose was too broad and my face too round. It took me a while to feel comfortable going to photoshoots. Despite the rejection, I was still willing to keeping modeling because I could see how hard work could lead to success. I continued to model until my husband came home from Vietnam in March 1967.

I had rented a two-bedroom apartment at 621 Hancock Street for ninety dollars a month in Bedford-Stuyvesant, an all-Black neighborhood. Our brownstone was a two-story building made of sandstone. Our apartment was on the second floor, and another family lived downstairs. I bought a new green/beige sofa and a dark-brown wood bedroom set. And, I paid cash for it—I remembered my dad did not believe in buying things on credit.

Soon, I started growing flowers on the back porch like my mom. I called it our dream house in Brooklyn because it was our first place together, our new beginning. I hung African wall art in the bedroom that my husband bought for me in Harlem. I kept flowers on the coffee table to bring gratitude and love into our home. Usually, I shopped at the A&P Supermarket around the corner and bought Joseph his Eight O'Clock Coffee, which he drank every morning for breakfast with his over-easy eggs. Since I was the baby in Aberdeen, Mary and Momma had fixed my meals, so though I was good at making coffee, I had a lot to learn about cooking. Joseph's eggs were often brown on his plate, but he ate them anyway. One day, I bought calf liver to steam in the pan and make gravy. But when I looked at that wet meat, I thought, *I can't cook that liver. Instead, I'll just warm up a TV dinner for Joseph.*

c❍

When Joseph had been home from Vietnam for two weeks, he saw my portfolio on the dresser. He browsed my photos and then told me, "You look amazing!"

"Thanks, Honey!" I grinned. "You remember that I wrote you about modeling with my friend, Nancy."

Joseph's expression changed. "I don't recall anything about you modeling." His voice got deeper.

He stood up, and with his hands clenching the chair, he continued loudly, "Estell, you are being exploited. I guess that you don't know that."

He grabbed my arm and said, "I came eight thousand miles to be with you. Now, you are modeling someone else's clothes and neglecting me." Abruptly, he grabbed his cap and left the room, slamming the door!

My stomach churned; I never seen my husband so fired up. I thought, "It's time for me to be assertive, and I am earning my own money. Why should there be a limit to what I can achieve? I want to share responsibility with my husband and receive equal respect."

I had never argued with Joseph, and I was feeling scared.

I thought about my momma. She was hardheaded. She worked, cooked our meals, and washed our clothes. But Momma always grumbled and complained. My dad was the breadwinner and made the decisions for the family. This was the tradition back then, and the culture was different for women in the 1950s. I recall the television program *Father Knows Best*, which was supposed to be the perfect family.

I heard Buddy barking, so I knew Joseph was in the kitchen. Soon, he marched into the living with two tall cups of sweet tea. I saw those brown eyes gazing me.

"I had time to cool down, and I am sorry that I got so upset," he said. "You can continue modeling."

I was surprised that he agreed to support me.

Joseph had been possessive of me since I first met him. I hugged him and mumbled, "We are a good team together." Modeling made me feel important because it paid well, and I could shop at any store on Fifth Avenue. When my husband left the military in July 1967, I decided to quit modeling and spend more time getting to know him since he'd left for Vietnam two weeks after we were married.

⌒

Joseph stayed in the army for about another six months after his return from Vietnam. During his three years in the army, he was stationed at Governors Island, Fort Bragg, Fort Knox, and Aberdeen, Maryland. I went to a couple of those army bases as his wife.

He received an honorable discharge in July 1967. The day he arrived at the San Francisco Airport from the jungle in Vietnam, he heard the song "California Dreamin'" by The Mamas & the Papas. On the plane, he read the *Los Angeles Times,* and he saw the antiwar protesters in the airport. He was dejected because his best friend, Josh, had been killed by a grenade while they fought together. Joseph was happy to be home to see his family, but seeing all that disrespect for veterans was unsettling for him.

Once he was discharged, it took about three months to get a job because there were so many negative articles in the press about the war. Many businesses would not even consider hiring a veteran. Finally, he was hired by the postal service in Manhattan, sorting mail and a desk clerk. After the war, several Vietnam soldiers from his unit visited him. They were like brothers who had trust and respect for each other. One of his friends was named Cash Dollars; he was a tall white guy with blue eyes from New Jersey. And another friend was Jacob, who was short with a bald head and lived in Harlem. They often stayed for hours talking to Joseph about taking care of his family. Joseph and his friends discussed the adjustment to a new life, but the common threads were their service in Vietnam and how difficult it was to find work. That was the case in 1967 no matter what race you were.

Many veterans like my husband were stigmatized as being on drugs while in Vietnam and thought to be unable to fit into the workplace. Because the war was so unpopular, it took months before Joseph and Cash Dollars were hired. His friend Jacob had a family; they were homeless and slept in their car. Finally, his church helped him get an apartment for his family.

11
Awakenings

~~~∂~∂~O~~~

ALTHOUGH I GREW up a lot during my early days in New York, my real transformation was yet to come.

When I first got to New York City, I had negative feelings about how I'd been treated because of my skin color, and I was quiet and insecure. In Mississippi, there were so many rules I had to follow to stay safe. For example, when I went shopping at the dime store with my mother, I had to call the cashier, a sixteen-year-old white girl, "Miss," and I was told to keep my gaze down and not look her in the eye. This was puzzling to me. When I bought my toys, Momma and I had to wait until all the white customers were taken care of first before we received service.

I had a sense of freedom in New York because I saw people who looked like me express their opinions in the community. Joseph helped me realize that my voice and my perspective were important. Joseph was bold because his family had lived in Sugar Hill, an historic neighborhood in Harlem where he witnessed his neighbors owning their businesses and living "the sweet life." From that time on, I questioned who I was and why.

Joseph knew more about his history than I did because he had access to the Schomburg Center for Research in Black Culture. He read books about Jackie Robinson, who integrated baseball, and Bessie Coleman, a pioneer in aviation. As Joseph shared our cultural history, I began to understand my identity. Our conversations about jazz great John Coltrane and Afro-American journalist Ida B. Wells were enlightening. I remember thinking, *This guy is smart.* And he introduced me to the Harlem Renaissance and its rich history. He told me stories about Langston Hughes and recited "Dream Deferred." I enjoyed our conversations, and Joseph liked talking about our ancestors in Africa and the Caribbean, and I never heard anyone speak of our people with such admiration and respect.

The Black Power movement started in 1960 and became a rallying cry for new ideas. The movement emphasized economic and political empowerment as well as racial pride, and it introduced a renaissance of ideas and cultural awareness. On the radio, James Brown's "Say It Loud—I'm Black and I'm Proud" made us proclaim our identity. For the first time, I was proud of my brown skin. Music was politically charged at the time, and I witnessed a change in both attitudes and labels: I was no longer Colored or Negro … I was Black. Although my ancestors came to this country as slaves, that label did not define who I was.

In Bedford-Stuyvesant, I was aware of the common interest we shared, like having a safe neighborhood and keeping it clean. When I looked in the mirror, for the first time I saw my dark skin with a glow of love. There was a commonality in the community. Black women wore their hair in a loose style with its natural texture or braided. I experienced a shift in my beliefs about my appearance; now, I saw my brown skin and my textured hair as attractive features.

Soon I bought my first daishiki with a yellow and blue tunic on Nostrand Avenue about two miles from our home. Next, I headed to the Jama beauty shop to transition to my natural hair journey. I waited ten minutes at the hair salon. Suddenly, my stylist, Sofia, invited me to sit in her chair.

"Hi, Estell," Sofia greeted me and said, "the receptionist said you wanted an Afro." She massaged my scalp and then proceeded to wash it.

I brought my own bottle of herbal shampoo with honey for her to wash my hair. Sofia cut and styled my hair, and after just forty-five minutes, she handed me the mirror. I saw my short, thick Afro reflected in the oval mirror. I felt pampered and energetic. I stood up, grabbed my shoulder bag, and thanked Sofia.

After I left the beauty shop, I browsed the store windows of the shops nearby, thinking, "Joseph is going to be excited to see my natural look." I bought a pair of gold hooped earrings, Afro combs, and T-shirts emblazoned with the image of a fist. I shopped at these local Black-owned businesses because they had merchandise that I could not buy on Fifth Avenue.

My Sister Comes to New York

In August 1967, my sister, who looked like me with short, curled hair and cheekbones like our daddy, visited me in New York. She was my spiritual twin. We shared our bedrooms growing up, and like most sisters, we also had our times of bickering about me wearing her clothes. When I went to Shivers High School, Mary put makeup on my face, rouge on my cheeks, and that wild cherry lipstick on my lips when I was sixteen. I remember peering into the mirror for hours. I could trust her about things I couldn't ask anyone else. One time, I asked her about kissing boys, and she just giggled with that shy smile of hers, and I don't remember her answering my question.

I rode with Cousin James to pick up Mary and her family at the Port Authority bus station on 8th Avenue in Lower Manhattan. I ran to embrace her as soon as she stepped off the bus. I hugged six-year-old Gregory, who was missing two front teeth and had wavy hair. And her husband, Tom, tall like my husband, grasped my hand while saying, "Hey, we made it to New York."

I introduced them to Cousin James, and then we headed to the old Cadillac with its tailfins, which was parked near Forty-Second Street and Eighth Avenue. When Mary stepped onto the street near the station, she held her son's hand tightly. She kept looking at the tall skyscrapers and the yellow cabs racing down the street. Her eyes glassy, she mumbled, "I have never seen a city like New York."

Soon, the Cadillac was moving through Midtown to our apartment on Hancock Street in Brooklyn, where Joseph was sitting on the steps. He stood quickly and rushed to give Mary a big hug. Mary said, "I am so happy to meet you, and your voice sounds heavy, just like over the phone." Joseph shook hands with Tom and met my nephew Gregory Sims, whose nickname was Robert. And finally, they all met Buddy, who sniffed around the family. Gregory loved rubbing Buddy's tan fur.

Mary settled into the small bedroom with new yellow curtains that I stitched on my Singer sewing machine to bring back memories of our shared childhood. I stayed up many nights with my sister when I was a ten-year-old to learn how to thread a needle for sewing and use a Vogue pattern. Mary was patient; I was stubborn. *Now, she will be stunned when she sees these curtains*, I thought.

I had invited my sister and her husband to come to New York to check out the neighborhood and to see if they wanted to live there. After they saw the shops were within walking distance and the subway was just down the street, they decided to stay in New York. Indeed, I encouraged them, and Joseph offered to help them find jobs.

After three weeks, Mary got a job in a clothing store on Prospect Avenue in Brooklyn, and Tom worked at a warehouse in Queens. On weekends, Joseph and Tom took the subway to Harlem to hang out with friends and watch the Knicks games. The subway was two blocks from home; it cost only thirty-five cents. Saturday was usually our day for shopping. Mary and Gregory would dress up, and we'd walk to the subway station. "Hurry," I'd tell them, "Let's take the A Train."

In Manhattan, we sauntered into Lord & Taylor on Thirty-Eighth Street near Fifth Avenue. This store had rows of purses and dresses, and my sister said, "I have never seen so many clothes in one place." She picked a new blue dress and matching shoes on that trip as I recall. We stopped on the street corner for New York-style pizza, and Gregory got an orange, Italian ice.

Most Sunday afternoons there was a family gathering in my small kitchen. Mary prepared her golden-brown biscuits, and I fixed the collard greens and red Kool-Aid. Of course, my sister cooked the fried chicken with brown gravy. As Joseph smacked his lips on the chicken, he told Mary, "You know how to cook! Estell is still learning," and they all giggled. Mary wore her apron and baked a carrot cake and topped it with thick cream cheese icing. It was so yummy and moist.

On Saturday night, September 9, I had a surprise birthday party for my sister. I went into Mary's bedroom and told her that guests are waiting for her in the living room. "Why?" she asked. "Because I am celebrating your birthday," I told her with delight.

She followed me into the living room, where we begin singing, "Happy Birthday, Mary." I had baked a coconut cake with pineapple filling for her, and she blew out the candles. There were balloons hanging from the ceiling, plenty of loud clapping, and a bouquet of roses from her husband. The music of Marvin Gaye singing "I Heard It Through the Grapevine" serenaded her from the record player. Gregory gave his mom a big pink card and a hug. Tom, Joseph, and the neighbors watched as Mary open her gifts. Later, my sister told me, "Sis, you really made that cake? It was so good that I devoured two slices." She gave me a bear hug.

One day after they'd been in New York for four months, Mary and I were sitting on the red couch in the living room when she told me they were returning to Aberdeen. I was flustered because I knew how much I would miss her, especially our all-night chats.

"Okay, then I am taking you on a walking tour of Harlem," I said, "and you will see the historic Abyssinian Baptist Church on 138th Street where Congressman Adam Clayton Powell is a Baptist minister.

"I heard about him on the news," Mary said in awe.

"I know that you've missed Momma, Daddy, and your friends," I uttered. "I want you to be happy. Did you tell Gregory? Because you know how much he likes his friends at the prep school."

"No," she said. "Not yet, because he really loves New York."

I took a deep breath and then quickly told her, "Well, I am pregnant! And I did not tell Joseph yet. I am scared."

Mary got the biggest grin on her face, and she scooped over and squeezed me tightly. "You're going to be a great mom," she told me.

By the next Saturday, the family was all packed with their suitcases sitting by the front door. I sat to talk with my nephew, and he had tears in his eyes. "Aunt Sis," he said, "I'm gonna miss New York and playing chess with Uncle Joseph." I put my arms around him, and Mary sat beside me. Tom stood near the fireplace and patted Buddy on the head. Joseph walked into the living room with his tall cup of coffee and asked, "Have y'all been crying?"

We took the subway with them to the Port Authority, and I cried as the Greyhound bus pulled away with my sister and her family. Afterward, Joseph and I rode the Eight Avenue subway home. We sat in the seat with our hands locked together, tucked by the window in silence. Mary's visit will always be etched in my memory.

$\backsim$

One Wednesday morning in September 1967, I was putting together a breakfast of hash browns, poached eggs, and beef bacon with a tall mug of hot chocolate for my husband. Buddy sat in the kitchen with us, barking out the window. I settled down in my chair at the square table with my cup of green tea and waited for Joseph to finish convincing Buddy to calm down. As he rubbed Buddy's ear, I took a deep breath and announced, "Joseph, I am pregnant."

Joseph jumped out of his chair and yelled, "My wife is going to have a baby." Then he wrapped his arms around me and caressed my shoulders. "Estell, I had only dreamed about this moment."

"Joseph, you are going to be a dad," I said, still not quite believing it myself. "Well, I'm three months pregnant."

When he asked if I was feeling all right, I admitted I was feeling nauseous.

"Is that why you are not eating your breakfast?"

"I suppose that my body is adjusting."

"Why didn't you tell me right away?" Joseph asked with concern.

"At first," I admitted, "I was scared, but when I told my sister, she told me I would be a great mother, and a feeling of bliss washed over me."

"Listen, Estell, I have to rush off to work," Joseph said as he got up to leave. "This weekend, I'm taking you out for dinner to celebrate."

That Saturday morning was cold and windy, and I wore my boots and hooded jacket when I went down the street to Mabel's beauty shop to get a manicure with red nail polish, new eyelashes, and my textured short haircut. My new hairstylist from South Carolina made me look amazing. I feel happy when I am looking good.

At 8:00 p.m., Joseph had his beard shaved neatly and was dressed in his blue suit and tie. He insisted that I wear that new light-blue dress from Gimbel's that he had picked for me, and I paired it with my Chanel N°5 perfume. When we were finished getting ready for the evening, I was a pampered princess filled with confidence and style. I was wearing my invisible crown. Joseph knew how to nurture my spirit. We exited the brownstone, and Joseph hailed a cab.

While I sat in the back seat with Joseph holding my hand and humming, I reminisced about the skyline with the bright lights and traveling across the Brooklyn Bridge. The next stop was the Hilton Hotel near Central Park. I peered up at the forty-seven-story tower and thought it was undoubtedly fabulous. As the Yellow Cab stopped in front of the hotel, a concierge dressed in a black uniform greeted us and opened the door.

We sauntered up the steps and into the lobby, which had chandeliers and gray carpet, and white roses filled the entrance. Soft piano music played in the background. Joseph held my hand firmly as we rode the elevator with an attendant to the second floor.

Joseph had that New York swagger like a man with a mission. He told the maître d' at the podium, "Reservations for Mr. and Mrs. Halliburton." We followed the man to our table; the refreshing smell of the eucalyptus permeated the air. Gliding to the table, I remembered the time when I was eight years old in Aberdeen that Momma told me to watch my manners. I admired all the linen tablecloths and sparkling silverware in the room as we walked toward our table, and I thought *If Momma could see me now!* as the maître d' assisted me into a comfortable lime-green chair.

Our waiter arrived quickly, and Joseph ordered a glass of wine but reminded him, "No alcohol for you, wife." While Joseph sat there holding my hand and I looked at elegantly rolled burgundy napkins on our plates, I kept wondering how he could afford this fancy restaurant. I thought we were saving our money, but I did not want to spoil our special night.

My husband and I finished our cheese and garlic bread appetizers. Then, we dined on T-bone steaks with red potatoes and a Caesar salad.

At the end of our meal, while I sipped my tea, Joseph said, "I want a cultural name for our baby."

I agreed with that idea and added, "If it's a girl, I might want to name her Estell. Yet, I am willing to consider an ethnic name."

"How do you like the name Fatima?" Joseph asked. "That's a beautiful name."

"Well, let me think about it," I said.

Joseph looked into my eyes. "We are going to be family, and you are my angel." From his jacket pocket, Joseph pulled out a silver jewelry box and showed me the gold necklace inside, which was engraved, *Joseph and Estell. Our legacy will live forever.* My eyes welled up with tears. Joseph moved his chair closer to me and rubbed my stomach. "I can't wait to see our baby," he said softly.

The waiter returned carrying a silver tray with a tall slice of cheesecake with two big strawberries and whipped topping. As he placed the dessert in front of me, he announced, "Congratulations, Mom!"

"Thank you!" I turned to my husband. "Joseph, I will remember how you made me feel so special." After we finished our celebration dessert, we took the elevator to the first floor of the hotel, and the concierge hailed a cab.

I had dined at the best restaurant in New York wearing my new dress … which was already getting tight; I had gained a few pounds. But all I could think about was how happy I was. I knew our lives would change with the birth of our first child, but I had no idea how much they would soon change in other significant ways.

12

Our Next Chapter

I WORKED FOR TWO years in the accounting department at Gilbert Carrier on Thirty-Fourth Street. When I first came to New York in 1965, I went to a small business school in Manhattan. I took classes in clerical office duties, which included being a stenographer; that enabled me to transcribe spoken words into written documents. My first job in Aberdeen was as a maid, at fourteen years old, and I cleaned and mopped floors to earn my own money. My job at Gilbert Carrier offered better pay, and I enjoyed working with a team. But when I worked in a professional office, I saw that women got paid less and worked longer hours than men. Even though I was trained in clerical work, I still had to brew coffee and pass out the donuts in the office.

Gilbert Carrier was within walking distance of the Empire State Building. On Fridays, I usually went out to lunch with my coworkers to celebrate the end of another busy week. I enjoyed eating curried fish at the Indian café and sesame chicken at the Chinese restaurant. While growing up in Aberdeen, I never dreamed of sampling so many diverse cuisines from other countries.

I was friendly with my coworkers, especially Rachel, who was Jewish. When I celebrated my birthday in March, my coworkers brought me sponge cake with sliced strawberries. Rachel, who told funny stories about her younger sister, gave me a yellow gift box and embraced me. I just stood there in surprise. Had this white girl just hugged me?

Rachel asked, "Estell, what's wrong?" Growing up in Aberdeen, I wasn't used to being touched by someone with a different skin color—and smiling, too.

It had taken a while to feel a real connection with Rachel. As months passed, I began to really like her. She and I shopped for shoes and jewelry at B. Altman on Fifth Avenue. And on several occasions, she brought fresh bagels with cream cheese for us to share. Then, I baked a sweet potato pie for her. Afterward, she asked me to bake a pie for her birthday. Finally, I saw her as just another kind friend. Soon, she met Joseph, who she thought was handsome.

Another friend, Camilo, who was from the Caribbean, worked with me on journal entries. Often, she came to visit me on Saturday afternoons. We sat on thick green pillows while watching James Bond movies. She usually brought green grapes and fresh-baked pretzels for our snack. Camilo fell in love with Buddy, our puppy, and fed him bite-sized treats.

Camilo reminded me of my friends in high school with her positive attitude. I told her about bumping into my classmate Octavia from Tuskegee University while walking on Forty-Second Street. Octavia and I screamed and hugged each other for five minutes. I took a step back in time that day.

By December 1967, I was feeling the magic of the season. People singing Christmas carols on the street corners and the colorful store windows at Macy's put me in the holiday spirit. While shopping for my work wardrobe, I looked at knitted pink sweaters and daydreamed about my baby girl.

It took weeks to find professional clothing for work. Finally, I purchased new maternity clothes from Lane Bryant at Thirty-Ninth Street near Fifth Avenue because I was getting bigger—I was six months pregnant. Wow, my baby was growing. As a result, my work wardrobe had changed. Months earlier, I'd worn a size six, but I was wearing a size fourteen by December. I had about four colorful outfits with matching shoes, which I wore to work in rotation.

In January 1968, Human Resources told me that it was a liability for me to keep working there once I was seven months pregnant, which was common at that time. The manager told me I could come back after my baby was born, but I had to resign. I did not think that it was fair for the company to make me quit. But the laws did not protect my right to work through my pregnancy. With this experience, I recognized the inequity of receiving fewer opportunities because of my gender.

On Friday, my last day of work at Gilbert Carrier, the ladies in the office had a surprise baby shower, including a beautiful pink three-layer cake, a tray of lemon drop cookies, cherry blossom flowers, and two tables of wrapped gift boxes. In addition, there was a stroller and a baby carriage from Macy's next to the table. I cut a big slice of my cake amid cheers. It was noisy with the clicking of forks and opening my gifts. My next surprise was Joseph walking in; my friends started clapping and shouting, "Dad is here!" My friend Camilo took our pictures with a Kodak Instamatic camera. After the celebration, I hugged my coworkers Rachel and Anya, who were good friends. Finally, after a group hug, and with teary eyes, I said, "I am going to miss you guys." Then, Joseph gathered the gifts, and my friends followed us to the Yellow Cab waiting on the curb. I waved good-bye, and as we pulled away, I thought, *This job has contributed to my happiness and raised my self-esteem. It enabled me to grow and make my own decisions.* I knew I would miss my work and my coworkers, but my life was about to change in a wonderful way.

I am standing at the mantle in our living room with my natural hair and wearing my striped maturity dress from Gimbels on Fifth Avenue, feeling joyful because I am going to be a mom.

I was five months pregnant and could feel my baby wiggling; it was a wonderful feeling. I thought that if the baby was a girl, she might look like me. When Joseph learned that I was pregnant, he was more than happy. I had never seen him so energetic, yet he was worried and kept a close eye on my swollen feet. I was on a new path of motherhood and asking advice from my sister, Mary. With my husband beside me, I knew that we would be great parents.

Welcoming Fatima

On March 16, 1968, Joseph rushed me to the hospital in a cab; he was carrying a suitcase that I had packed just for this occasion. My feet were swollen, and my contractions were about seven minutes apart. Joseph's voice was cracking and animated as he told the cabbie to hurry. With his arm around my shoulder, we entered Brooklyn Jewish Hospital on Prospect Place, and Joseph checked me in at the front desk. I was taking deep breaths to relieve my stress. I was sure that I was ready to be a mother, to hold my daughter in my arms and get up in the middle of the night!

On that cool Tuesday morning, the nurse told Joseph that he was not allowed to go back with me to the delivery room. With his lips curled, Joseph said, "I need to be with my wife!"

"Mr. Halliburton," the nurse said kindly, "I will take good care of your wife." Suddenly, Joseph squeezed my hand tightly and said, "I am praying for you and our baby."

I was not sure of what to expect for labor. This was my first baby, and the wrenching pain was overwhelming. The nurse pushed my wheelchair to room #3. All I could see were the white hospital walls and the rotating fan in the ceiling. The pain of contractions had me gripping onto my wheelchair. I screamed, "Can someone help me?" After I got to my room, I was transferred to a bed.

Once I was settled into my room, I saw Dr. Patricia Johnson, my gynecologist, who was smiling and holding my hand, which put me at ease. Minutes later, I was given a shot in my backside, and the numbing medicine was just what I needed to relax. The next thing I remember was waking up two hours later to my doctor saying, "Mrs. Halliburton, you have a baby girl!" My baby weighed seven pounds and ten ounces. She was a beautiful, brown-eyed girl with tiny fingers.

Soon, I was pushed back to my room, where the sun was beaming through the window. My husband and his mom came to visit me in my room. Joseph stood over my bed in a daze and caressed me. He held my hand as he stammered, "I saw our daughter … she has so much hair." Joseph had a fresh bouquet of yellow and pink tulips with a huge balloon. "I am a father," Joseph mumbled as he slumped down in the chair next to my bed.

After giving me a kiss, Joseph was quiet. Carrie sat by my bed and squeezed my hand. "I am so proud of you, Mom." She gazed at her son and asked him, "Joseph, are you all right?"

"It was exciting to hold my baby, and she seems so fragile," he told his mom.

I told Carrie, "It was pure magic, and a new beginning for us." Then I realized how I must look. "Carrie, I need a mirror. My hair is sticking up on my head."

"Listen," she said, "you look fine. I brought your bag with your makeup and hair combs." But I wanted to look put together. I began brushing my hair and putting dabs of Royal Crown hair dressing on my scalp. The skin-care counter at the J. C. Penney department store didn't offer makeup for darker skin tones, so I had to use powder that was a shade lighter than my skin. Still, I wanted to look elegant for my picture with my baby girl.

Our family sat together for a few minutes in silence. Finally, Carrie asked, "Did you think of a name for the baby?"

Joseph answered. "I think that we will name her Fatima. It's an Islamic name, which will allow her to have her own cultural identity.

"That's a beautiful name." Carrie nodded her approval. "I know your daughter will cherish her name."

When I look into my daughter's eyes, I thought, *I believe she will represent our family values and continue our quest for equality.*

After three days in the hospital, Joseph took us home. My stomach was still swollen, but I was relieved to be going home! I said, "I am stepping into motherhood."

∽

Our first weeks at home were blissful. I dressed Fatima in her white braided cap and sweater and sat her in the middle of the bed. I could barely take my eyes off her, and my husband talked to our daughter for hours.

My momma, Estell Sims, came to visit from Aberdeen, she liked our Brownstone apartment which was upstairs. She was excited to see her granddaughter. When Momma walked into my living room and embraced me, she looked totally amazed.

"Sis, what happen to your hair? You have changed!" she said.

"I know, Momma, and I am wearing an Afro. I cut my hair short."

I told Momma that I remembered the days in our kitchen when she straightened my hair; I could still smell the burning scent of the hot comb. "My daughter will never endure those feelings," I told her. "I am happy with my natural hair." Then I modeled my red African print dress that was a way to connect to my ancestors.

Momma shook her head and twisted her hands. "I guess you been influenced by your husband," she said.

"Yes, I agree with him about social justice."

"Never mind, I am glad you married a good man."

From her suitcase, Momma removed a blue gingham dress for me and pink blankets for the baby. As I watched her hold my two-week-old baby, my face lit up with smiles. And the next morning when I woke up, I heard my mother and Joseph giggling in the kitchen. I was relieved that Momma was friendly with my husband. Joseph was different from those guys I dated in Aberdeen who were clean-shaven and quiet. Joseph always stated his opinions.

During my momma's visit, my mother-in-law, Carrie, came to see her. They were both from the South and around the same age. They talked about boiling chitlins (the belly of a hog) on the farm and eating crackling bread. My momma, Estell, complimented Carrie about her son, saying she liked that Joseph was a good father and had provided a good home for her daughter. Carrie cradled Fatima in her arms and said, "I love my granddaughter." Momma chimed in with, "I am so proud of my daughter Sis."

Listening to them chat, I was as giddy as a teenage girl. There were times that Momma and I butted heads, but I remembered all the years she took care of me, like when I had the measles for ten days and she sat by my bed for hours. On Friday, Carrie took my momma to 125th Street in Harlem to see gospel singer Clara Ward perform "Time Is Winding Up" at the Apollo Theatre, and Momma came back happy. "I was clapping and waving my arms and forgot about my white purse," she said. "You know what, Carrie held it for me."

For two weeks, my momma just latched onto Fatima. Her visit was special for us. Before she left for Aberdeen, Joseph and I took Momma to Times Square, and she uttered, "New York has too many folks on the streets," yet she liked the subway. With her visit, my mother made me feel like I was a woman now and that she respected me … I knew that she really loved me.

A New Beginning

Just a few weeks later, on Thursday, April 4, 1968, I was in the kitchen holding Fatima and admiring the pink daisy blooming on the window-sill. At 6:00 p.m., I carried her into the bedroom to watch the local news on WABC on our small black-and-white television. Breaking news soon interrupted the program, and Walter Cronkite said, "Dr. Martin Luther King, the apostle of nonviolence in the civil rights movement, has been shot to death in Memphis, Tennessee ."

I cradled my baby tightly in my arms, with my lips pursed and my eyes glued to the screen. Cool spring air blew through the window, yet it seemed like the room was spinning. I listened to the reports about Dr. King's assassination and viewed the pictures of the Lorraine Motel. Everything about it was so shocking.

In Aberdeen, I had witnessed Dr. King going to jail in Birmingham in 1963 because he was protesting racial injustice. In August of that year, in his "I Have a Dream" Speech at the March on Washington, he stated, "I will not be judged by the color of my skin, but by the content of my character." When I heard that message, I felt a spirit rise inside of my body.

Now I thought, *Our leader has been cut down, and what's next?* I thought about the pervasive racism in my life since my birth on the plantation.

Hours passed by, and I couldn't move … my body was stuck with my red throw around my shoulder as I gazed at my two-week-old baby. My puppy, Buddy, laid his head on my lap.

The thick green telephone rang on the side table; it was Joseph.

"Hey, are you and Fatima all right? I heard the news on the radio about Martin Luther King, and I am so angry and full of rage. I am going to make sure that you and my baby are safe."

"Joseph, calm down, and we got each other."

"All right, I am in a phone booth, and I am getting the Seventh Avenue subway. See you soon, my love."

At 8:00 p.m., I heard Joseph's footsteps striking the stairway. While waiting for him, I drank Lipton hot tea on the green couch in the living room. Joseph marched into the room and shouted, "I can't believe that Martin Luther King is dead." His eyes flashed with anger, and his face reflected his raw emotions. He slowly took off his jacket, and then he walked over to us, bent down, and squeezed us tightly. "I'm worried about our future," he mumbled.

Our pain just glued us together. We just sat in silence for hours with our baby wrapped in her pink baby quilt.

Later that night, there was rioting about six blocks from my home. I heard sirens passing for hours. On the news, reports stated that three people had been shot in the riot on Nostrand Avenue. There was so much anger everywhere because Dr. King was dead, which sparked widespread protests in my neighborhood of Brooklyn and in Harlem. This was a reckoning of our hurt and frustration for all the years we had been denied our rights.

In the morning, I prepared a cup of coffee for Joseph and put cream cheese on his blueberry bagel. As we sat together contemplating the events of the night before, Joseph rubbed his head with his hand.

Finally, he said, "Estell, we've got to make a change. When I was living in Washington Heights, my friend Thomas, who was thirteen years old and lived down the hall, was arrested for stealing a purse and dragged from his apartment with a bloody nose. His mom ran down three flights of stairs while crying and yelling, 'Please, don't hurt my boy!' For years, I did not realize that the police could arrest a young boy. Eventually, he was released from jail because they had arrested the wrong person. His life was never the same. I've lived with that image all of my life."

I thought of my sister, Mary, and me walking to town on Saturday morning and seeing three young white men in a pickup truck with a Confederate flag. They slowed down to throw rocks and bottles at us. Mary and I ran like two rabbits because we were scared, knowing how much hate these men had for us because we were not white.

⁂

That spring, the American civil rights movement to end systemic racism was well underway, but many Blacks felt the movement did not settle our demands for justice. Joseph had seen blatant racism with poverty and menial jobs for Black soldiers. He had served his country, and he was distressed over the daily inequalities he witnessed and experienced.

Joseph had told me about listening to the speeches of Malcolm X on 125th Street in Harlem when he was a teenager. Now, Joseph began talking about the Black Panther Party, a revolutionary group organized in 1966 by Huey P. Newton in Oakland, California. Joseph like that he preached Black self-reliance and standing up for our rights. In Aberdeen, segregation was so restrictive that I was too frightened to protest because I knew I could be beaten or jailed. I did not know how to challenge segregation; therefore, I was full of anger when I shopped in the stores and my parents were denied the right to vote.

Joseph decided to become a member of the Black Panther Party because he liked the Panthers' demands for justice. The Panthers, whose members wore distinctive leather jackets with black berets, broke from the integration and nonviolence goals of the civil rights movement. They challenged the police and the white establishment with their demands for equal justice and an end to police brutality. In 1967, they began publishing *The Black Panther* newspaper about the racial struggles in minority communities. There were women in the Black Panther Party who marched with the men, and they were in leadership positions too. The Black Panthers were popular in our urban neighborhood because they were willing to challenge the police.

One of the Black Panther chapters was on Fulton Street in Brooklyn, and Joseph joined with thousands of other young black men and women. As a member of the Black Panthers, Joseph spent long hours helping to clean up the piles of garbage in the neighborhood. And he aided with setting up a breakfast program for young children in Brownsville (a neighborhood in Brooklyn). Joseph marched with the Panthers to city hall because his friend Lucas was shot and killed by the police. On several occasions, the Black Panther office on Fulton Street was raided by police to undermine the group's leadership. There was no outcry for justice because Black lives did not matter in 1968.

When Joseph joined the Panthers in 1968, I was scared. I knew that this was my time to take a stand with Joseph, and I supported him, yet I was always thinking about the danger he faced.

After Joseph left the military, he was deeply troubled by the equities he saw in our neighborhood and in the workplace. He remembered the lessons he learned from his dad in Harlem about young Black men being stereotyped as criminal and lazy: "Son, you got to obey the law or risk going to jail." Joseph was annoyed when he thought about his identity as a Black man. At twenty-four years old, Joseph wanted to be a good husband and protect our family. As he watched the Black Power movement unfold, he decided that Islam could give meaning to our lives.

My husband, Joseph R. Halliburton, was twenty-six years old in this photo. He was six feet tall, with glowing brown skin, muscular shoulders, and heavy eyebrows, and a thick mustache and beard. I was fascinated with Joseph because he carried the history of our race in his head. I wasn't sure of my identity as a Black woman in 1965, but my husband helped me learn and embrace my history.

Joseph and I were different, with him being a Leo, the lion with a loud voice, and me a Pisces, the fish with a mild tone of voice. I was infatuated with this guy from Harlem, who became a Vietnam veteran, a Black Panther, and devout Muslim as well as my husband and life partner and the father of my three beautiful girls.

In May, Joseph's friend Ibrahim invited us to join the mosque. I wasn't sure that this was the right thing to do, but I was willing to find out. One of the people who really influenced us about Islam was Muhammad Ali, the heavyweight boxing champion, who said, "I am America. I am the part you won't recognize." He continued to inspire us when he said, "I believe in the religion of Islam." Ali, a cultural icon, spoke with such love about being a Black man and in defiance against the system of racism.

We took our oath at the mosque from the Imam, Rashad, who led the worshipers. I met his wife, Sister Halima, a woman with a kind smile who was dressed in a beautiful light-blue dress and a headscarf. I chatted with her about my family, and she assisted me with learning my prayers in Islam. The Iman then gave us the Quran, the sacred scriptures of Islam with the teachings of Muhammad, wrapped in a velvet cloth.

Muhammad was an Arab religious leader and the founder of Islam. He was the last prophet and was sent to confirm the teaching of Abraham, Moses, and Jesus. The text in the Quran is about kindness, resilience, and living in gratitude.

While at the mosque, we met people from all over the world who recognized our values and worshipped together. Even though I did not speak their languages, I was in a caring and loving atmosphere. I wore modest clothes like a headscarf and dresses below the knees, and Joseph wore a knitted beige prayer cap. One of Islam's principles involved eating healthy foods and no pork. It took me a while to stop eating honey brown ham, but I changed my eating habits.

We prayed five times a day, and Joseph bought us matching green Persian prayer rugs, which we placed on the floor where we kneeled to pray. Soon, we learned about Jumu'ah, the worship service that was held every Friday.

Joseph just beamed with enthusiasm while at the mosque, and he made many new friends. He often spent weekends learning how to speak his prayers in Arabic, and he knew them within a couple of months.

Joining Islam was a good decision for Joseph and our family. Islam became the ethical framework for our daily life. Joseph began really listening to my ideas about our finances. Furthermore, he supported us getting together with other families from the mosque. I saw more harmony in our lives, especially when we prayed together.

Moreover, I saw a change in his attitude about me as his wife and about the family. I would go shopping on Saturday and come home to find Joseph had ironed his shirts for work. *Something has changed with my husband*, I thought. He was getting up at 2:00 a.m. and feeding our daughter her bottle. At breakfast, he mentioned that he wanted to buy a house in Queens and start his own business. Indeed, I had confidence in him. My husband treated me like I had a crown on my head. The recognition of being a wife and a mother showed that my husband valued our relationship.

❧

Before I joined the mosque, I changed my hairstyle. A very short Afro suited my new vision of being a woman of color. Joseph grew a beard, and he wore a thick, towering Afro. Joseph bought me a new wardrobe from a boutique in Harlem, and I looked beautiful in my red maxi dress with an African print. My friends noticed a change in my wardrobe. My next-door neighbor Jo Ann saw me in the yard, and she asked what happen to my straightened hair. I told her, "I am wearing my natural hair to express my authentic personality." "I am not ready for this social justice movement," she answered. I realized then that some people of color struggled with all the changes that were happening.

13

Visiting Aberdeen

~~~~~~

I T WAS AUGUST 1968, and I was excited about our visit to
Aberdeen. This would be the first time Joseph had been south since
he was ten years old and visited his grandma, Sadie Halliburton,
in South Carolina.

At 5:00 a.m. on a windy Friday morning, Joseph loaded our suitcases into the trunk of a rental car, which was parked in front of our
brownstone on Hancock Street. It was a red Buick Skylark from Avis
with a black-and-red interior and flashy cherry-red seats. I had dressed
Fatima in her pink hand-knitted sweater set, and she was cocooned
in her car seat with her rattle. I wore my long, yellow floral-print
dress with puffy sleeves and carried a tote bag, which dangled on my
shoulder. I also wore a beaming smile because I was sure my momma
would be pleased when she saw my new dress.

Not surprisingly, there was heavy traffic on the George Washington
Bridge. Joseph flipped the dial on the radio to WOR-FM, and we
listened as Ella Fitzgerald, the leading lady of jazz, belt out "A-Tisket,
A-Tasket" as we left behind the tall skyscrapers for the road to my
hometown. I remembered that when I first came to New York on

that Trailways bus, it was a two-day trip, and my legs had ached from those tight seats. This time, I was sitting in the passenger seat of a cozy car with my husband.

"It's a twelve-hour drive," Joseph had said. Perhaps Fatima, who was six months old and had two teeth, would sleep most the way. I stashed her pink teddy bear beside her and Cheerios in my lunch bags to keep her happy.

○

On the highway and crossing into Tuscaloosa, Alabama, we saw horses in the corral, cows in the pastures, and roadside vegetable stands selling watermelons. I saw a field with budding cotton that reminded me of my years on the plantation. We passed a bulldog barking in the yard of a small wood-frame house with a woman sitting on the porch. A few miles down the road, Joseph had to hit the brakes for a chicken crossing the gravel road. He mumbled, "I feel like I'm in another country." I'd forgotten to remind him that sometimes the young hens fly out of the coops and run free, just like my momma's chicken in Aberdeen.

Turning the pages of his wrinkled map book, Joseph said we should be in Aberdeen before 7:00 p.m. Yet we still had miles to travel, so I turned the silver dial on the radio and stopped at the FM country music station.

Joseph had a surprised look on his face. "Estell, you never told me that you like country music. I'm learning something new about your life."

"Yeah, when I was little girl, I got accustomed to listening to country music because it was the only music on the radio in 1955. It took me a while to get the melody of the music. On a good day, I could hear Fats Domino singing 'Ain't That a Shame,' and gospel hymns on Sunday mornings," I reminisced. "I also listened to the music of Johnny Cash about life and hard times. Further, I would hum 'I Walk the Line.' And I listened to Patsy Cline's 'Crazy,' and I thought she had a good voice, too.

"It's good music," I told Joseph. "Moreover, I am fond of the blues with BB King and Muddy Waters. I hummed these songs while sitting on the porch with Spooky, my dog." It was fun to share those memories with my husband.

As we drove along, Joseph kept going over the speed limit, and I reminded him that we were in the South. "You know that your mother warned you about being stopped by the police," I reminded him. "I want you to drive within the speed limit."

"Estell," he assured me, "I will slow down, and I am not afraid of the police."

"I know, but please listen to us," I pleaded with him.

"Okay, I got it!" he said. He squeezed my hand to reassure me.

The sun was still shining as we headed into Mississippi on Route 45, passing through Tupelo and Amory, Mississippi, and crossing the Tombigbee River Bridge. In grade school, I learned the name "Tombigbee" is a Choctaw word meaning "box maker." (The Choctaw are a Native American tribe.)

I glanced at Joseph, who was wearing silly green sunglasses that his brother had given him. Joseph chuckled. "You're giving me a history lesson about the South on this trip. Who knows, one day we might live in the South!"

"Well," I said, giggling, "I prefer the city life."

"I'm just a little scared to meet your dad," Joseph continued. "He lived through segregation with such courage, and I consider him an unsung hero."

I smiled at the thought of my husband and my dad meeting. "My dad is a proud man who works six days a week," I bragged. "Just keep that charming look and say, 'Yes, sir' when responding to my dad's questions."

Arriving in Aberdeen

Joseph maneuvered the red Buick up the hill on Commerce Street and obeyed its one stoplight. I saw McDuffie Drug, a wooden building where Momma used to buy her medicine, and Kimmel Bakery with its faded sign on the window. The thought of those fresh cinnamon rolls made me lick my lips. Down the street was Elkin Theatre, where *Gone with the Wind* probably played during its historic run. And there was Aberdeen's City Hall with its marble steps. At ten years old, I ran up those steps to see my dad, who was the janitor for many years.

My dad and his brothers in Aberdeen were hard workers. Jason was a butcher, Roosevelt provided maintenance for the school system, and Curley was a landscaping contractor. The four men were leaders in the Colored community. They owned their homes and were deacons in the church. Moreover, these brothers belonged to the Masonic lodge. They dressed in suits and ties for Sunday church service.

My daddy knew the mayors and the chief of police, and he could talk to the prisoners—the Black men—in the jail at city hall and give messages to the families. Daddy helped keep Cousin Boog from being arrested for running the red light by using his influence with the chief of police. My Uncle Jason helped Colored folk who were sharecroppers get food on credit at Hussey's general store. Despite the Jim Crow laws, these brothers knew the people that mattered. When I went to school, my friends would ask, "Is your daddy Wardell?" "Yes," I'd answer with pride, "that's my dad!"

As we drove through town, I pointed out places to my husband where I went shopping with my momma while growing up. Aberdeen is unique and has its own identity: quiet, with magnolia trees and antebellum homes and good people. The folks enjoyed front yard BBQs and picnics, and you might even see a refrigerator on the front porch. Bluegrass bars with plenty of catfish with hush puppies were favorites. Gospel music played on the radio on Sunday morning along with preaching, and somebody was always getting fried chicken ready for the preacher after church.

Aberdeen has its own cultural heritage of music, too, thanks to the music of B. B. King, known as the "King of the Blues," who was born about 125 miles away in Itta Bena, Mississippi. He became famous for his song "The Thrill Is Gone."

I remembered going to church at Pilgrim Rest. It was an old wooden church building on Franklin Street. The choir sang "This Little Light of Mine" for Sunday service, and sometimes they were out of tune, but I still clapped to the music. The windows were hitched up on warm days, and big fans rotated the air. The women looked good even with sweat rolling down their cheeks.

Momma looked put together every Sunday, dressed in a rimmed pink hat with feathers, a white suit with gold buttons, and leather heels. Of course, she wore Avon perfume with the flowery smell of roses, which followed her everywhere, and she carried her Bible in her purse. My sister and I wore colorful dresses and walked with our shoulders back and heads held up high. My daddy was a deacon at Daniel Baptist, which he attended with his brother Curly on the south side of town. When we first moved to Aberdeen, Momma decided to attend Pilgrim Rest Church because it was within walking distance of our home, but they often attended church together. The church was a place where Colored folk could feel free to express their feelings and be treated with respect.

But whites and Blacks lived separate lives.

I recalled a day when I was ten years old and my dad had given me $2.00 for my allowance; I was so happy. My sister, Mary, and I went to Elmore's Dime Store on Commerce Street.

I wore my yellow sundress because it was sweltering hot that afternoon. Mary was looking at handbags in aisle 3, and I was chewing Juicy Fruit gum and had a big smile on my face. In the next aisle, I picked out a silver bracelet that cost $1.99. I strutted to the counter to pay the cashier. The young white girl said, "What are you doing in this line? Didn't you see that sign for *Colored*, little girl?" I dropped the bracelet on the counter and scurried over to my sister, yelling, "Let's go."

"Sis, what's wrong," Mary asked with concern.

"Nothing! I want to go home to my momma," I told her. I just balled up my fists and bit my lips. I remember leaving the store and my sister running after me.

Although this happened years ago, I still feel weak and empty inside when I think about that day. I often ask myself, *Who was this young girl to talk to me that way? When did she learn to hate me?*

Many times, my daddy walked to Tony's restaurant on Commerce Street for a burger since he worked at city hall, but he always entered through the back door. We lived in a segregated neighborhood, and we attended the Colored school with used books and scratched-up desks. Our football field, which was near a burning garbage dump, had poles for the goal post. In contrast, the white school had new books, a brick school building, and a football field with a goal post and freshly cut grass. I tried to ignore my place in Aberdeen as a Colored girl, but racism was not only part of the landscape, it was ubiquitous.

Homecoming

Joseph parked the red Buick in front of 308 Matubba Street, my home. The two-bedroom white house had black shutters and a paved walkway; a magnolia tree grew adjacent to the porch. Momma scurried off the porch to greet us in her flannel dress. I opened the door of the car and unbuckled Fatima from her car seat. Momma hugged me quickly and grabbed my baby, and said with delight, "I am holding my grandbaby. And, Sis, the baby looks like Joseph, really!"

My husband put his arm around Momma's shoulder, and I left in search of my daddy, who always sat in his recliner in the evening when he wasn't working. I stepped through the back door and across the linoleum floor through the living room. Suddenly, I was nervous thinking how my daddy would feel about my husband when he met him for the first time. I was sure Daddy thought that I would marry someone from the South. *But I am a woman on my own journey,* I thought.

I turned the knob on the bedroom door. The pale-blue bedroom with the chifforobe, the rotating fan, and the small black-and-white TV had not changed. Of course, Daddy's Bible rested beside him on the small table, and next to his chair was his orange-colored cat, Kitty. Then I saw Daddy's square face. He was wearing his overalls, and his black-rimmed glasses were perched on his nose, and nothing else mattered. I just remember clutching his body and hugging him, and Daddy mumbling, "Sis, I am so happy that you are home" and patting my back.

My eyes welled with tears because I felt a tight bond with my dad, something I'd felt since I was little girl on the plantation. When I left for New York, he thought I was too young to travel there alone, but rather than criticize me, he supported my trip.

"Sis," he repeated, "I am so happy that you are home with your family." Then he inspected me.

"What happened with your hair?" he asked.

"I decided to get an Afro and lose my curls."

"Sis, you have changed since living in New York," Daddy said.

"I found my voice living in the city and feel confident about my family," I told him proudly.

He smiled while removing his black-rimmed glasses, and then Joseph knocked at the door. Daddy told him to come on in, and he stood to shake hands with my husband. "Son, I am glad that you are here," he said to Joseph. Then they embraced each other. At six-foot-four, my dad stood taller than my husband, and he was lean with the arms of a bodybuilder. Watching these two significant men in my life standing together was an unforgettable moment. I wanted us to share our lives.

Before I left the room, Daddy told me, "Sis, bring us two bottles of Coca-Cola from the small refrigerator."

"All right, I'll let you guy talk."

As I left the bedroom, I could hear Daddy asking Joseph about his family and telling him, "You look like your picture with that Afro." When I returned with the Cokes, my dad asked Joseph about his service in Vietnam, and Daddy mentioned my brother, Alfred, who died in Korea. They talked for about an hour.

Joseph came back to the living room with a smile. "What did Daddy say?" I asked anxiously.

"Well, he seemed concerned about us embracing Islam. I assured him that my family comes first and our religion is about serving God, and I shared my sincere intention to care for my family. He told me, 'I am happy that you are part of this family.'"

I smiled. "Joseph, I forgot how charming you can be at times."

Then Joseph saw my band picture on the wall over the couch. "You were kind of cute in your band uniform," he teased me.

"I remember my clarinet squeaking on the front porch when I practiced out there with our cat, Kitty. I told him. Next, I told him to come and look at my pink bedroom with the ruffled curtains. I pointed out Mary's picture on the dresser, in her polka shirt. I shared about the time I had gone on a date at Shivers High School and ended up crawling through my bedroom window because I came home late and really hoped my momma did not wake up.

My husband shook his head. "I cannot believe you did that."

"That is a secret between me and my sister," I told him. Wiping sweat from my forehead, I plugged in the rotating fan, and then told him I needed to check on Fatima because she might be hungry. Joseph gave me a kiss on the cheek and then said, "I'm going to unpack my bags and put on my Converse sneakers."

Momma was rocking my daughter on the front porch that over-looked her azaleas. These flowers around the walkway still reminded me of us digging holes to plant roses. I told her that Daddy was waiting to see his granddaughter. I picked up Fatima, who was clutching her pink teddy bear, and carried her inside.

Daddy was still sitting in his comfortable chair in the bedroom. When he saw Fatima, he reached out his arms for her, and his eyes glistened as he cradled his new granddaughter.

My dad, Wardell Sims, and his granddaughter Fatima. In 1968, I went back to Aberdeen with my husband, who was meeting my family for the first time, and our new baby, Fatima, who was six months old. This picture was taken in the back yard on Matubba Street with my dad, who was about sixty years old and dressed in his Sunday clothes after church at Daniel Baptist. Daddy just smiled and made a fuss when Fatima cried. He loved Fatima, who he called *Fatma*. She was special because, he said, she reminded him of me. He held Fatima for hours while she drank her bottle with her yellow teddy bear. Fatima wore a light pink dress with a bow on her braided hair and white sandals.

"Sis, I can't believe that you have a husband and a baby," he said, his voice a little hoarse. "I am so happy to hold my granddaughter, and she has two teeth. Sis, she is looking at me with those brown eyes." My daddy couldn't take his eyes off my daughter. I left the room with a wide grin on my face.

Next, I chatted with Momma in the living room, where we sat together on the green vinyl sofa. She wanted to give me advice about taking care of my daughter.

"What kind of milk is Fatima drinking? She should be drinking Carnation milk," she said.

"Momma," I said, "I am breastfeeding my daughter, and she drinks Enfamil formula. I am grown woman, and my baby is healthy. I appreciate your concern. However, many things have changed since I was a baby on the farm." I knew Momma just wanted the best for her grandbaby.

Later, I followed Daddy when he headed outside to feed Kitty.

"Richard seems like a good man," he told me. Richard was Joseph's middle name. "Where did you get that name for the baby?"

"It is an Islamic name," I explained.

"Is Fatma ..."

"You almost got it," I said with a smile.

"Now that I've met your husband, I believe he is a good man ... but I do think he should cut off some of that hair."

"I like his urban look," I told him, "And this is the culture in New York." I decided to change the subject. "So, Daddy, I see you getting some gray hair, yet you still put a new roof on the house."

"Sis, I don't know how to slow down," he said.

I was so proud of my daddy. "I want to be like you when I'm sixty-five and get up every morning at five a.m. Have you ever thought about retiring?"

He didn't even hesitate. "No, I will work until God calls me home."

Before bedtime that first evening, Tom, Mary, and Gregory came to visit. Joseph greeted the family, and we sat in the living room as he told them about the chickens on the road. It was a lively conversation. Then I stayed up half the night talking with my sister, and I spent the next day shopping with her at Big Star Grocery.

On Friday evening, my uncles came to visit, and my aunts brought pork ribs and BBQ chicken for a celebration in the back yard; Fatima was the center of attention. Mary's strawberry cake and Momma's apple turnovers were freshly baked. I knew I was having an extra helping of desserts. And Momma prepared collard green with smoked turkey since she knew that I had stopped eating pork. I was pleased.

After a week, I was not ready to go home, but it was time to leave. Joseph was thrilled that my dad liked him. Fatima was spoiled after being with her grandparents. For our trip home, Momma packed baby blankets and shirts for her granddaughter. Daddy had Kimmel's chocolate fudge in a square white box for me.

Joseph had put our belonging in the trunk of the Buick. It was time to leave Aberdeen, and there were lots of hugs for my daughter and my husband. I embraced my parents with teary eyes, knowing how much I treasured them.

14

Love Makes a Family

⁓꙳⁓

WHEN WE ARRIVED home on a breezy Sunday night after the twelve-hour trip from Aberdeen, we got settled into our apartment, and I grabbed our mail. Joseph went next door to get Buddy, who was staying with our neighbor, Jo Ann. Fatima was asleep, so I put her to bed. I was too tired to unpack our bags, but I called my mother to let her know that we were home.

The next morning as Joseph was leaving for work, he expressed concern that I wasn't eating my breakfast.

"I'm not hungry today," I told him. "I'll eat with Fatima.".

Joseph planted a kiss on my cheek. "I will call when I get to work, love you!"

On Friday morning, my friend Camilo called on the phone and asked me to check out the Crunch Fitness gym on Bedford Avenue with her on Saturday morning.

I agreed to the plan. "I need to lose weight because I tore into that fried chicken in Aberdeen, and I couldn't resist the Sugar Babies either," I mumbled. I told her that my husband had run circles around me on the two-mile run at Prospect Park in Brooklyn the month before. He was bragging! I wanted to shut him up, so I said, "I think Joseph would babysit Fatima."

Camilo said, "I got these new Converse shoes and a running suit, and I am ready to do push-ups and squats. We can join the yoga classes with a little meditation, too. Estell, I need to get in shape! I'll see you on Saturday!"

⌒⑤

One Friday night in November, I sat with my family in the living room listening to Fatima singing the ABC song. She said in her sweet little voice, "Mama, sing with me." I chimed in with my voice cracking. Soon Joseph made us a bowl of popcorn to relax on the sofa, but Buddy kept barking and pulling on the sofa pillows. I didn't feel well while nibbling on the popcorn, and I told Joseph that I had a stomachache and had taken some Pepto Bismol. I admitted to him that I did eat spicy wings the day before. Joseph suggested I get an appointment with Dr. Harris.

I went to see my Dr. Harris the next day. After a thorough examination, she said, "Mrs. Halliburton, you are pregnant." I was a little surprised, but I was extremely happy that a new baby was growing inside me.

I couldn't wait to tell Joseph when he got home from work. He strolled into the bedroom where I was sitting in the swivel chair.

"Estell, I was worried about you all day," he said. "Are you all right?"

"Joseph, I am pregnant!"

His expression turned from concern to joy. "My wife is having a baby," Joseph hollered.

I tried to shush him by telling him, "Hey, you are too loud."

Joseph held my hand, and we strolled to Fatima's room. The three of us huddled together on her small bed. Joseph cradled Fatima in his arms and told her, "Your mommy is having a baby."

"Oh, baby," Fatima said. She rubbed my tummy.

As we sat together, Joseph reminded me about the Islamic names we had discussed. "If it is a girl, Rabia," he said, "and if it's a boy, Omar."

"I like the sound of these names," I responded. Then I told him, "I am calling Carrie and my momma in Aberdeen."

∽

A few days later, Joseph called from work and told me that he was taking me to dinner since Fatima was spending the night with her grandma. When he walked into the living room after work, he carried a big bouquet of long-stemmed red roses. As Joseph handed them to me, he said, "This is for you, Mom." Then with a wide grin on his face, he said, "I got tickets for a Broadway show. It is the play *A Raisin in the Sun* by Lorraine Hansberry. It's at the Centre Style Theatre on Fifty-Fifth Street."

I put on my thick green wool coat and suede boots, and Joseph insisted that I wear an extra scarf because it was only fifteen degrees outside.

Our first stop was Mamma Leone on Forty-Fourth Street, where I enjoyed the skinny Italian noodles with eggplant red sauce for dinner. After dinner, Joseph hailed a taxi in time for the show, which started at 8:30 p.m.

The small theater seated about 300 people, and our seats were in the center; we were so close to the stage that I could touch it. Once the curtains opened, my eyes were glued to the performers. Seeing a live play on stage about the dreams and struggles of a Black family in an urban area felt like a ninety-minute fantasy, and Joseph kept squeezing my hand and smiling.

∽

I was excited about our family growing. By Thanksgiving, my belly was getting bigger, and walking upstairs was uncomfortable. However, I enjoyed going to Rockefeller Center to see the 75-foot-tall Christmas tree with its hundreds of silver lights, with Joseph holding our daughter. I can recall some of these details because I was writing in a journal about the wonderful life that I would have with Fatima and our new baby.

◦◯

On a Saturday afternoon in March, Joseph took Fatima and me out for lunch. I had told my husband that I just wanted to stay home. I was eight months pregnant with swollen feet, but he insisted on taking us out. When we returned to our apartment, I slowly walked up the stairs holding Fatima's hand.

"Mommy," she told me, "I hear noise inside."

Joseph said, "That's probably Buddy, our puppy." He opened the door.

I heard clapping and Jasmine's voice telling me, "Welcome to your baby shower, Estell!" I looked around my apartment to see crepe paper ribbons and bows of pink and yellow and blue hanging from the ceiling with huge balloons. A table in the middle of the room held a white cake decorated with pink baby shoes. On a second table were gifts, which I opened while my guests watched and told funny stories. I opened a gift from Camilo, which was a handmade baby blanket, and a big box from Carrie with a baby bouncer in it. I just kept giggling. Each gift lifted my spirit, and I just thought about my precious baby.

I thanked my friends, coworkers, neighbors, and family, including Cousin James and Ruth, for an amazing shower. I was happy to see the celebration of my baby because I never had gifts like this when I was a baby.

◦◯

On Wednesday, April 29, 1970, we welcomed our second daughter. This time we picked the Islamic name Rabia, which means spring, *a new beginning.* She was a muscular baby with long legs and thick, curly hair who weighed eight pounds. Rabia was born at Brooklyn Jewish Hospital on a cold, windy morning around 4:00 a.m., and Dr. Harrington delivered her. I was calm, and so excited that Fatima would have a sister; I was looking forward to being a mother to my two girls. Joseph ignited with joy, and he had a new swagger in his walk.

The nurse brought my baby to me in what looked like swaddling clothes. I held my baby tenderly to see her sweet face; Rabia was so precious. Joseph touched her tiny hands. Finally, he said to me, "Listen, Estell, can I hold my daughter, Rabia?"

"Yes, you know that's *our* daughter, Joseph," I said with a smile as I handed her into his waiting arms.

Just then, Joseph's younger brother, Herbie, came to see our baby. I advised everyone to wash their hands before touching my baby. Herbie whispered, "Can I hold my niece, please?" Joseph told him, "You got to wait your turn." I babbled, "Grandma Carrie should hold the baby next."

Carrie cradled our baby, cooing to her, "I am your granny, and I love your round cheeks, Rabia."

Finally, Herbie got his chance to hold his niece.

Carrie had brought along two wrapped gifts for her new grand-daughter from Bloomingdale's on Fifty-Ninth Street off Third Avenue. There was a white knitted blanket with pink bows and a light blue dress with booties. Joseph handed me pink candy roses and a white robe with *Mother* printed on it. It was so soft; I winked at him.

After three days in the hospital, I missed Fatima, who was not allowed to come to the hospital because she was so young. Joseph took me home with our baby girl. I knew Fatima would be happy to see her sister.

On Saturday morning, I came home from Brooklyn Jewish Hospital with Joseph carrying my suitcase and a bunch of flowers. My arms were tightly wrapped around my sweet daughter, Rabia. I missed Fatima, who was staying with my friend Jasmine, and I was sure she wanted to see her baby sister. While I was rocking Rabia, Jasmine came into the bedroom with Fatima, who was wearing a light blue jacket and cap. I thanked my friend for taking care of my daughter, and she chuckled, "Wow, that's a pretty baby girl."

I called Fatima to "come and see your sister." I waited for her to run to hug her baby sister. Instead, two-year-old Fatima just stood there in awe with her hands gripping her yellow blanket; she looked scared. I suppose she thought that another baby had taken her place.

Joseph rushed to our daughter and said, "I love you, Fatima" while picking her up. Then, he brought Fatima to sit on my lap with me and our new baby. I told Fatima to give her sister a hug, and she leaned back into me. With Rabia cuddled in my arms and Fatima on my lap, I was gushing with joy.

Fatima took a while to warm up to the idea of having a baby sister around, but after about a week, she held Rabia's hand and gave her a kiss on the cheek. Over the next weeks, Fatima came to love her sister and called her "Baby Sister."

Once I was holding two babies, I was busy all the time! But I loved the attention and the drooling from baby Rabia. Joseph would come home early from his job at the post office to rock our girls, but I don't know how I would have made it through those first months if it hadn't been for my mother-in-law, Carrie.

My Mother-in-Law, Carrie

When I first met Joseph's mother and father in October 1964, I was impressed. They had been married for thirty years. Joseph (Jack) and Carrie Halliburton lived in the Bronx at a six-story apartment building. My husband was named after his dad, who maintained the building as a manager. His dad reminded me of my father, who believed in working long hours. And Joseph's dad, an army veteran, motivated my husband to join the military.

Carrie was always like a mother to me in New York. She was quiet, and tall with high cheekbones. She had culinary experience and had worked for families on Long Island, but she was retired when I met her. When I was first introduced to Carrie, I thought she had an attitude because she was quiet and kept her face blank. When I asked Joseph later if he thought his mother liked me, he said, "Yes, she told me that you wore colorful clothing that fits you and with matching earrings. My other girlfriends never impressed her." The next time I visited her home, she told me she thought I was courageous for coming to New York.

In addition, she mentioned that she never dreamed I was from the South. When I asked her why not, she said, "I guess because you speak with such confidence." Obviously, I was stunned!

Carrie had assisted me in shopping for my first maternity dress at Gimbel's on Thirty-Second Street. After we finished our shopping, we rode the subway to Chock full o'Nuts near Fifty-Ninth Street for lunch. Carrie ordered a cinnamon twist with green tea for our snack. As we chatted, I explained to her that I enjoyed writing in my journal and reading poems. Carrie mentioned Shakespeare and quoted lines from *Othello*. I was astonished. I told her about learning the epic story of *Beowulf* in high school and how it took me a while to grasp the narrative. Carries was familiar with the story, and I was amused by her passion for literature. "Joseph did not tell me that you liked the classics," I told her.

"Last week," I continued, "Joseph shopped at Kizzy's bookstore near Amsterdam Avenue and purchased *The Fire Next Time* by James Baldwin, and this author can tell a story like you're in the room."

Still sipping her tea, Carrie said, "You know Baldwin grew up in Harlem, and I've read all of his books." I was certainly impressed with her knowledge of different genres of books.

Since the days of slavery, grandmothers have helped maintain their family histories with oral stories to carry on our legacy. I did visit my grandma, Mary Jane Pruitt, with my mother and my sister when I lived on the plantation. Grandma Pruitt lived about three miles from my family in a one-room house on another plantation. She was short like my momma and walked with a cane. I recall she nicknamed me "Cutie," and I sat with her on the porch swing. I liked playing with her fuzzy gray cat, Moon, when we visited. Years later, after we moved to Aberdeen, she died of a stroke when I was eight years old. I wish that I could have spent more time with her.

I was happy that my daughters would get know their grandmothers. From Carrie, I gained wisdom. And I knew her legacy would continue through my daughters.

One Saturday evening, Carrie came over to prepare a meal for our family. The table setting looked like something out of *Good Housekeeping* magazine. Our apartment was filled with the smell of fresh herbs, and she wore her pink apron while she pureed vegetables for her granddaughters. The kitchen was her territory. When she prepared the dinner, I got ready for a long wait—like four hours! It had to be perfect.

Finally, Carrie yelled, "Dinner is ready"! After an appetizer of curried dip, we feasted on spinach salad, Cornish hens, rice stuffing, and marinated Brussels sprouts. But the most elegant part of the meal was the four-layer rainbow cake with its blue, green, yellow, and red layers and a thick, creamy buttercream icing. I cut two slices for me and a hefty piece of that moist cake for Joseph. When her grandchildren saw the cake, they bounced in their seats and yelled, "Grammy!" Fatima and Rabia finished the cake with sticky fingers, icing on their braids, and crumbs on the floor.

Over the years, Carrie spent many hours sitting on the floor with pillows reading to Fatima with Rabia in her lap. Children's books in those days with stories about Black families were rare, and those that existed contained buffoonish images. Therefore, Carrie used images from *Ebony* and made small books for the girls. She wanted her granddaughters to love their identity. Other times, Carrie made cookie-cutter sugar cookies with them. The kitchen was a mess with Rabia sampling the dough with her fingers; Fatima liked the sprinkles. Carrie was a wonderful grandmother!

I came to love Carrie, so I was devastated when I learned she was ill. One day when Fatima was about six or seven months old, I heard Joseph in the kitchen one day talking to his mother on the telephone. "When is your next doctor's appointment?" he asked her. Soon, he hung up the green wall phone and turned to me.

I looked at his tight lips and asked, "Joseph, what is happening with your mother?

"My mother has stomach cancer."

I couldn't believe my ears. "How long have you known?"

"She told me about six months ago," Joseph admitted.

"You did not tell me!"

"Well, you seemed so happy with our new daughter. I just couldn't speak about it."

I walked over to where my husband sat on a stool near the window and squeezed his shoulder. He looked so dejected.

"Estell, I don't understand her having stomach cancer, and she might die soon." He was lost in thought for a minute and then smiled sadly.

I added, "This is such heartbreaking news." I had a sudden thought. "Then I want to go with your mother to the doctor." Joseph shared that she was going to the Memorial Sloan Kettering Cancer Center on East 67th Street for therapy.

"I want to make sure Carrie knows that she is not alone," I said and then sighed.

A faint smile flashed across my husband's face. "I am happy you are supporting my mom."

Carrie never let on how sick she really was, but once I knew about her cancer, I was determined to use every opportunity to fill her life with joy.

One Special Evening with the Queen of Soul

In June of 1971, Joseph decided to surprise me with a special celebration because I was exhausted from being up all night with our girls while he worked two jobs; in addition to his primary job at the main post office in Manhattan, he sold African paintings on the weekends.

One Friday evening, Grandma Carrie came to visit. Thirteen-month-old Rabia had four teeth and was just learning to walk. Fatima always kept her sister busy playing with ABC blocks on the carpet. Carrie rang the doorbell around 6:00 p.m. When I greeted her, she was standing in the doorway and holding two plush white teddy bears for our girls in her arms. Joseph had asked his mom to babysit her granddaughters for the evening. After we chatted for a moment, she strolled into my daughters' pink bedroom, and Fatima hollered, "Grammy!" as she ran to hug her. Rabia babbled "Nana" from her walker and waved her rattles. Carrie adored her granddaughters, and they loved the way she sang, "I'm a Little Teapot." However, I did not want to leave my daughters that night because I knew I would miss cradling them in my arms.

At 7:00 p.m., Joseph arrived home, and he walked into the bedroom with two tickets to see Aretha Franklin at the Apollo Theatre. When he showed them to me, I started bouncing around near my closet, yelling with excitement. I hugged Joseph, and then I began pulling out dresses from my closet and asking his opinion about which I should wear. He suggested that I wear my new blue maxi dress with glitter on the sleeves and my matching headscarf from the boutique on 145th Street. *All right,* I thought, *I do want to look elegant.*

"Joseph, after the concert, I want to stop at Sylvia, the historic soul food restaurant in Harlem on one hundred and twenty-sixth street," I told him excitedly. "All right," Joseph agreed, nodding, "we can definitely stop at Sylvia. I guess my mom told you about their chicken and waffles." Of course, Carrie had suggested it.

Joseph snapped on my pearl necklace, and I sprayed just a dab of perfume on my arm like my mother taught me. Joseph looked handsome with his fitted blue suit jacket, and the smell of Old Spice permeated the room. Carrie approved; she said, "My handsome son and charming daughter, I know that you will enjoy Aretha."

We cuddled the girls and embraced Carrie. On our way out the door, Joseph mentioned that Jasmine and her husband Noah were joining us for the concert. I was even more excited to share the evening with our friends.

As we walked to the sidewalk, a long black limousine pulled up; and the chauffeur stepped out to greet us and open my door! "Joseph, I thought we were taking a cab," I told him, "And you didn't tell me!" He flashed a smile. Joseph had amazed me again!

The chauffeur, who was dressed in a dark suit, was polite. Once Joseph and I were settled in the backseat smiling at each other and holding hands, I thought, *Wow, I am riding in a limousine. I'll never forget this night!* The driver picked up Jasmine and Noah, who lived on Putnam Avenue in Brooklyn. Our friendship had been strong for several years, and we both had families. But the theme of that night was Aretha!

The black limousine wound down the road and crossed the Williamsburg Bridge while I sipped on a glass of sparkling water and chatted with Jasmine. I told her that Joseph had bought me the "Lady Soul" album. Jasmine said wistfully, "Your husband is really thoughtful. I have to remind Noah about my birthday." I told her I was sure that his forgetfulness wasn't intentional.

I struggled to contain my excitement as I anticipated seeing this superstar. I remember reading in the *New York Times,* "Aretha Franklin,

The Queen of Soul, has captured the attention of the Apollo." In June 1971, she had a five-day concert series to sold-out crowds. The billboard at the Apollo read simply, "Welcome Home Aretha." She was an American singer and songwriter and a civil rights activist. And I believe she embodied the courage of a strong woman with her song "Respect."

In Harlem that June evening, sweat creased my forehead in the sizzling air. The lines of people were wrapped around the block, with buses and cars honking their horns. Harlem was ready for Aretha. As we entered the Apollo Theatre, displays of Ella Fitzgerald and Stevie Wonder lined the walls.

I recalled how, when I first came to New York, I went to the Apollo Theatre on amateur night with my cousin and Jasmine. Years later, here I was with my husband, and we were looking fine! Our seats were at the lower arena in front of the stage. The opening acts were a few dance routines. The audience was wired with excitement. At 8:30 p.m., the announcer's voice boomed, "Aretha Franklin, the Queen of Soul."

As Aretha entered the stage, the audience screamed, yelled, and whistled for what seemed like five minutes. She wore a sparkly, sequined red gown and glittering red heels. She commanded the stage with her band as she belted out, "You Make Me Feel Like a Natural Woman." This song was magic for me because I thought of self-love and making my own decisions.

Women stood in the aisles, hollering, "Aretha!" over the thunderous applause. Noah and Jasmine were standing and cheering, too.

Her next song was "Think." I had listened to so many of her songs on the radio that it was like listening to a friend. She was the voice of our culture and of what it felt like to be a Black woman. The gathering at the Apollo was like a family get-together. Joseph stood next to me while we clapped our hands, and he whispered, "I love you, mother of our daughters." I just beamed a big grin, happy to be there with my husband this time.

The concert lasted for ninety minutes, and I did not want it to end. Aretha wasn't just an entertainer; she was our role model. She touched my spirit with the lyrics from her songs. As a Black woman, she was telling our story in her music.

ᥩ

I decided to return to work in 1973, and I got a job on Nostrand Avenue in Brooklyn in accounting. I was unable to return to Gilbert Carrier because there were no openings.

I was looking forward to enhancing our income, but Joseph wanted me to stay home with our daughters. After we discussed it, he agreed to support me. One Sunday evening, I stayed up late in the living room drinking peppermint tea, and Joseph came to sit down with me.

"I know that you are worried about Rabia and Fatima," he said.

"Yes, I want to know how to handle going back to work and leaving my children during the day."

"Estell, you will adjust, and the girls are growing up," Joseph reassured me.

After visiting a couple of daycares, I registered Rabia in the Playhouse daycare on Halsey Street, and I met her teacher, Ms. Rainey. Fatima was already enrolled at the Brooklyn Elementary School on Marcy Avenue. I met her teacher, Ms. Garcia, who was patient and friendly. Fatima was happy to learn the basic skills of arithmetic and reading. I thought back to when I was her age and went to a one-room schoolhouse in the woods with my *Dick and Jane* book. I was often hungry with just a couple of biscuits to eat. I was grateful to know my daughter would be loved and would eat healthy lunches.

On Monday at 7:30 a.m., Joseph called to Fatima, who responded, "I'm ready to go, Daddy!" She was dressed for school in her two-toned saddle shoes and red jacket with her leather bookbag. Already dressed for work in my gray suit and two-inch heels, I stood near the front door and reminded Fatima to pay attention in class. I buttoned my daughter's coat and wrapped her knitted scarf around her neck. Then, I knelt to hug Fatima, and she waved goodbye to Rabia. Before they left, Joseph said, "Estell, you look amazing for your new job."

Once they were on their way to Fatima's school, I dressed Rabia in her corduroy pants, green jacket, and pink boots. I put her snacks of animal crackers and an apple in her lunch bag. Suddenly, I checked the clock and saw I was running late. I called my next-door neighbor, Jo Ann, to drop us off at the daycare.

The Playhouse daycare had a big yellow duck in the lobby. After the manager escorted us to Ms. Rainey's classroom, I removed Rabia's jacket and saw she was holding her white teddy bear. I told her that I was going to work. I cuddled my daughter and said, "I'll miss you, Rabia." At first, my daughter looked frightened. Then, she observed the children playing with puzzles. Rabia ran to sit with the other young children. So, I grabbed my purse, and Ms. Rainey, who wore her hair in a ponytail, smiled as she said, "Rabia is making friends." I waved goodbye to Rabia, feeling guilty for leaving her all day.

My eyes filled with tears, and I stopped in the bathroom at the daycare. I prayed for my babies to be safe. Afterward, I powdered my face, dabbed on pink lipstick, and headed outside to Jo Anne, who was waiting in the car. She looked at me and asked, "Estell, are you all right?"

"Yes," I said sadly, "please drop me off at work."

On the way, I realized I had never thought that the girls' transition to school would make me sad. *For the first time, I will be separated from my babies.*

⌒

Joseph liked the discipline that he experienced in the military. Like his dad, he was willing to sacrifice his life for his country, and he viewed his service as a test of his patriotism. My husband experienced prejudice in the military and saw the Confederate flag near his camp; many white officers rarely spoke about the Black troops. When Joseph returned home from Vietnam, he believed in standing up for his rights.

My twenty-five-year-old husband had doubts about the war; was it a just one? And he began to question authority. "Who is telling me the truth?" he'd say. When he came home, there were no victory parades, and society did not care that he had fought for his country in Vietnam. During this time, he was offered menial jobs even when he passed proficiency tests. My husband was disappointed, and I listened to him many nights as he shared the pain of his experience after Vietnam. At the same time, he was committed to our family and to growing as a father to our daughters.

Joseph had joined the Black Panthers, believing it was a political organization that could make a difference. Even though my husband was busy in the community, he still found time to read books like *Invisible Man* by Ralph Ellison, which tells the story of a Black man's journey to survive in our society.

One Friday, I saw my husband sitting on the green sofa in the living with the bills scattered on our glass coffee table and our dog, Buddy, lying beside him. Joseph was twirling his fingers and staring at his calculator. He looked unhappy and worried. I asked him what was wrong. He told me that he'd lost his weekend job.

"I was denied my raise after I had been there six months," he said. "Then, the manager said, 'This is your last day. I am sorry, but you still got your job at the post office.'"

"I know that you feel exploited on these jobs," I told my husband. "But one day, you will have your own business." And I truly believed that.

Joseph looked at me for a moment before he said, "You know how to make me feel special."

I massaged his shoulders and told him that we were going to be just fine.

"Estell, I know it is because we are a team," he agreed.

⚬

As a family, it was challenging to still live in our two-bedroom brownstone with two daughters. I enjoyed living in our brownstone apartment with its hardwood floors, and the rent was reasonable at $130.00 a month. But Joseph decided we needed more room, and I agreed. Joseph began calling real estate agents and checking out locations on Flatbush Avenue in Brooklyn. Those places were expensive, though, because we were looking at neighborhoods that offered a good public school and a place where our daughters could feel comfortable.

One day, he said, "My mother has a cousin in Los Angeles, and she lives near the beach."

"That sounds incredible, but it's too far from my mom and dad," I said. "I was thinking about moving south, maybe Atlanta?

"Estell, are you serious?"

Although I had mentioned it casually before, I spoke seriously this time to Joseph about moving to the South. When I first suggested the idea, I was just throwing it out there; I never thought I would seriously consider leaving New York, but we both were beginning to realize that we needed a change that would help us financially.

⚬

When I initially asked Joseph about leaving New York, he said, "I'll think about it." Just two days later, I overheard a phone call he had with his friend Lucas from the Black Panther Party. Lucas told Joseph that the police had raided the office on Fulton Street, and Joseph asked, "Do you think that I am in danger?" I couldn't hear the response, but

Joseph was quiet afterward, and his eyes were blank. I knew something was wrong, but Joseph never shared that information with me.

About two months later, the phone rang, and Joseph told me, "I am bringing home takeout. What do you want to eat?"

"Just surprise me, okay," I told him. Soon, my husband was marching into the living room where I was watching *Sanford and Son* on the small television, and he was followed close behind by Buddy, who smelled food.

While Joseph opened the bags and removed hot BBQ wings with bleu cheese and celery for me and a pastrami sandwich on marble rye bread with sauerkraut and mustard for him, I got Buddy's bowl for his treats.

Joseph's fingers were dripping with hot sauce when he looked at me and said, "Guess what, I decided to move south."

"Oh, my goodness!" It was all I could say. I hugged him tightly, and I dropped bleu cheese sauce on his yellow shirt.

"I always want to see you smile. Estell, you know that this is a lame idea," Joseph said in a serious tone.

I was so excited that all I could say was, "I will start working on our plan. My momma is going to be shocked, yet I know that she will be happy for us."

Moving back to the South was a scary thought. *Will my fear of change overshadow my curiosity? Will I lose what I have learned in New York?* I was worried that I would fall back into my old ways. Before, I pretended I was not affected by race, but after living in New York, I was aware of the disparity in my daily life.

Things were changing. Joseph said yes to moving to Atlanta. I would experience a slower pace in my life, and I was sure my family would adapt to the culture.

Moreover, my younger brother, Wardell Sims, lived in Atlanta with his family. Wardell had grown up on the plantation with our family. While on the farm, he went to the one-room house with our older brother, Alfred, my sister, Mary, and me. He loved to read; even when he went to the field to pick cotton, he hid in the bushes to read *The Catcher in the Rye* by J. D. Salinger with its torn pages.

My brother always told me to learn my times tables and stop watching Dale Evans and Roy Roger on TV. "You can't tell me what to do," had been my usual answer; I was hardheaded. Still, Wardell was always there for me, so I really missed him when he left Aberdeen for college in 1955 when I was ten years old. He gave me a red musical jewelry box that I kept until it didn't make any sound. I am so proud of Wardell, who graduated from Morehouse college in 1959. He inspired me to continue my education.

I phoned my brother to let him know about our plans to move to Atlanta. He said, "Sis I will help you and your family in finding a new home." I continued to have mixed feelings about moving because I really did not want to leave Brooklyn. I embraced living in a diverse culture. The thought of seeing the signs that read COLORED disturbed me.

15

Upsetting the Apple Cart

❧

ONCE JOSEPH AND I began discussing the possibility of leaving New York City and moving to Atlanta, it took about a month before we decided to move. About three weeks after that, we told our parents.

My husband told his mom right away, and she was dejected at the thought of not seeing her grandchildren. Next, I called my daddy to tell him.

"You're leaving New York!" Daddy said, "Sis, did Richard have a problem with the police?"

"No, Daddy! We decided to move to Atlanta because it is cheaper to live there and buy a home." Then, I talked to my mother, and she asked, "Sis, are you and my grandchildren all right?" I assured her we were. Before I hung up the phone, I tried to let them know that leaving New York would benefit our family. I was in tears after telling them and knowing they were worried about me.

Planning a Trip

One Friday afternoon, I stopped at the Village Café on Jefferson Avenue near our home. It was cold and windy, and I wore my brown boots and my heavy green coat with a fox-fur collar. The smell of freshly baked rolls filled the air as I entered the small restaurant, and I sat in the booth adjacent to the window. Soon Alonzo, the baldheaded owner, rushed to my table.

"Hello, Ms. Halliburton," he greeted, "your husband told me that you are moving to Atlanta. I'll miss Joseph. That's my partner for the Knicks' games at Madison Square Garden."

Soon, Joseph arrived at the restaurant, and Alonzo took our order. From the menu, I put in an order for two warm roast beef sandwiches with Swiss cheese on wheat bread with a Tab for me and a Pepsi for my husband.

Afterward, Joseph opened his leather zip folder and pulled out a thick notebook. "Estell, I wrote down a checklist for our move. I marked off the list that you are taking the girls to Aberdeen. I told my mother that we are leaving New York, and she just sat on the couch. She was despondent at the thought of not seeing her grandchildren. I've never seen my mom so sad."

"Well, I am taking the girls to spend the night with Carrie before their trip to Aberdeen," I told him. "Maybe the granddaughters can make her smile."

Joseph continued, "I asked my mother to keep Buddy because it will be safer for him. And my mother agreed to keep him."

I was shocked. "You mean Buddy is staying with your mother forever? Buddy is part of our family. I feel guilty leaving him here. And our daughters will miss Buddy tugging on them."

"Estell, I know that. It was a heartbreaking decision."

Suddenly, the restaurant got busy. Alonzo came with our sandwiches, plus kosher pickles and scalloped potatoes. Holding our plates,

Alonzo said, "I got that piping-hot chocolate lava cake waiting for you." I couldn't wait to taste it.

As we ate, Joseph mentioned, "Next on the list, we can put our furniture in storage and give some of it to our friends like Jasmine. I know my brothers, Anthony, and Herbie, will help us pack for the trip. I set up a time with United movers, and they charge by the hour." He took a bite of his sandwich.

"I told my boss at Pinkerton security that I am moving to Atlanta, and the manager is writing a good reference letter. When I hit the streets of Atlanta, I'll start my job search as a general contractor. Of course, I am trimming down my beard and Afro. I mean, I want to look more appealing to my employer."

While Joseph reviewed his list, I told him, "I will miss my accounting job in Brooklyn with my own desk. My coworkers found out that I am moving to Atlanta, so when I went to work on Monday, there was strawberry cupcake at my desk and a stunning bouquet of pink roses."

I doubted that I would get a clerical job in Atlanta. I told Joseph that the *Atlanta Journal* had jobs listed for Black women as salesclerks and cashiers for places like Rich's, a local department store. The minimum wage in Atlanta is $1.60 an hour, which was lower than in New York.

In addition, Joseph had been looking at the housing market in the *Atlanta Daily World*, the oldest Black newspaper in Atlanta. He saw places available in neighborhoods like Ben Hill, West End, Sweet Auburn, and Buckhead. He shared, "The apartments are cheaper than New York, at ninety dollars a month. I want to live in a clean neighborhood with friendly folk. I read most the areas are segregated just like in New York."

Next, I mentioned that I had our daughters' shot records, and they had received their last checkups with Dr. Johnson, their pediatrician. "She is giving me a referral for a new doctor. Also, I've informed Fatima's school and Rabia's daycare that our daughters are moving to Atlanta. My girls will miss all of their new friends."

We had finished eating by then, and Joseph put away his list. He looked at me with a gleam in his eyes.

"Estell, guess what? I bought us a car for our trip. My friend Ibraham helped me to pay cash for our new 1972 Impala. It has some miles on it, but no car payment."

"Joseph, I can't believe it! We have a car for our trip! You are a good hustler. When can I ride in our new car?"

"Our maroon Chevrolet is parked outside," he announced with a smile.

"Our prayers have been answered, Joseph. I am ready to go!" I hugged my husband in the booth.

Joseph grabbed my red scarf to put around my neck and assisted me with my jacket. I told him I wanted a takeaway box for our chocolate cake. He waved his hand at Alonzo and asked for a container for our cake.

My husband thanked Alonzo for the free meal, and we waved goodnight.

I strutted to the sidewalk where our shiny maroon Chevrolet was waiting, and Joseph opened the door for me. When we were settled, he turned over the engine and asked, "Where do you want to go?"

"Well, let's go to Times Square, and maybe you'll take me to that movie, *Buck and the Preacher* with Sidney Poitier, and buy us a big bag of buttered popcorn."

Joseph responded, "All right, let celebrate!"

Girls' Night Out with Grandma Carrie

Soon after, I took my daughters to spend the night with Carrie in the Bronx. I packed a small suitcase, and we rode the IRT subway train; the girls were bundled up in their pink boots, white jackets, and pink caps. As we headed to her apartment, the girls pointed out bicycle riders and a woman walking her bulldog. Soon, we were knocking on the door of Apt. B-1.

Carrie opened the door. She wore a green flannel dress and had her hair wrapped in a bun. My daughters lunged into their grandma's arms. Once we were all inside, she removed their coats. Then we sat on the couch with them in front of a bowl of yellow Goldfish crackers on the coffee table, and my daughters rushed to grab a handful. While I chatted with my girls, Carrie turned on the TV to *Sesame Street*. Fatima and Rabia moved to sit on the kids' yellow bean bags. They love the diverse characters on the show, including Big Bird and Kermit the Frog.

Once she got the girls settled, Carrie turned to me.

"My son told me that you are planning to leave New York and move to Atlanta. Estell, I am feeling sad just thinking about not seeing my grandchildren. What can I do to keep you and Joseph in New York?" Before I could answer, she continued, "I got an account at Chase Bank on Madison Avenue. You are welcome to my saving account." I was surprised, and grateful for her love for us.

"I appreciate it," I said, "but we are fine."

Carrie looked unconvinced." Joseph also added that you are taking the girls to stay with your mom in Aberdeen."

"Yes, I am," I told her. "Joseph bought our tickets. And I know that you are keeping Buddy for us. It's going to be sad to leave him, but I remember that you gave Buddy to me when Joseph was in Vietnam. Buddy, with his big brown eyes, kept me from being lonely, and I hope he'll keep you from missing us too much."

"Estell, I will enjoy keeping Buddy and taking walks with him," Carrie said sadly.

I didn't stay long after that. "While the girls are spending the night with you, I am going to the hairdressers." Carrie seemed happy, and mentioned that she would be making cut-out sugar cookies with Fatima and Rabia.

"You are spoiling them, again," I scolded her, but I was just teasing. "I wish that I could stay for the cookies, but my appointment for my hairdresser is in Brooklyn." I waved at Carrie and my daughters before leaving.

Joseph came with me to pick up our daughters the next day. It would be the last time that Carrie would see her granddaughters. When we entered the apartment on Saturday afternoon, Joseph's younger brother Anthony was sitting on the floor with our daughters, surrounded by stacks of blocks. Cousin Michael came out of the kitchen with a tall glass of iced tea.

"Hey, Richard and Estell!" Michael said when he saw us. "What's this I hear about you moving to Atlanta?"

My husband responded, "Oh yes, we are moving at the end of the month."

Michael looked surprised. "You are really leaving New York? Estell, I know that you convinced your husband to move."

"Well," I admitted, "I did suggest it. But I will miss you guys!"

Joseph stayed in the living room to hang out with Anthony and Michael. I headed to the bedroom to chat with Carrie about our trip to Atlanta.

Soon I heard Joseph holler, "Estell! Come and get your coat so we can take our daughters home." Carrie and I joined the others in the living room and started gathering up the children's belongings. Fatima and Rabia had new leather purses from their grandma, and teddy bears, too.

At the door, Rabia laid her head on her grandma's shoulder and Fatima tugged on her dress. "It's hard to separate from my family," Carrie said as she hugged them close. "I love my girls." Then, her eyes welled with tears as she handed Rabia to me. When Fatima saw her grandma's tears, she begins to cry.

I hugged Carrie. "My daughters will miss you," I told her as my voice cracked.

Joseph held his mother's trembling hands. "Mom, I am grateful that you came over to babysit and cook those fancy meals."

By that time, I needed a handkerchief to wipe my nose. We waved goodbye and left. As I stepped out the door, I told my husband, "I am so conflicted about leaving New York."

We were all feeling sad, so I suggested, "Let go get some strawberry ice cream."

Fatima and Rabia Leave New York

One evening later that week when my husband came home from work, we sat on the red loveseat in our bedroom with Buddy lying next to us with his paws on Joseph's lap.

"Joseph, you know that I called my parents about us moving to the South and asked them to watch our girls for a while. They happily agreed, but my mother was asking about us leaving New York. I told her I'd explain to her when I travel with the girls to Aberdeen.

"Joseph, I am excited, and I am nervous." I sighed. "This experience feels like I am on a roller coaster."

My husband reached to clutch my hand and said, "I am worried too. But I know our girls are going to be all right!"

We had decided I would fly with the girls to take them to my parents so they would be safe while we packed and moved. *Wow, this will be my first trip on an airplane*, I thought. I twisted my hands, wondering if it was safe to travel on a plane. I was scared because I like my feet on the ground.

"Joseph, did you get our Southwest Airlines tickets?" He told me that we were scheduled to leave on Thursday, April 11, and my roundtrip ticket cost $90.00. "Listen," he assured me, "once you get on the plane with our daughters, you will enjoy seeing the clouds in the sky."

The night of April 10 was a sleepless one for me. I was leaving my husband in New York and taking my daughters to Aberdeen. On that cold and windy morning of April 11, I packed the girls' clothes with their special blankets and toys. It was 7:00 a.m., and our plane would leave at 11:00 a.m. The day before, I had explained to my daughters that they would stay with their Grandma Estell in Aberdeen for a while. Fatima, who was six years old, knew that she was leaving New York. Rabia, at just four years old, wasn't sure what was happening.

Before our trip to the airport, Joseph got breakfast ready. He set the table in the kitchen with the blue-checkered tablecloth. As I flopped down in my chair beside my daughters, I saw a red rose near my plate, and I held its velvety petals to my nose. I nodded to my husband, who was busy preparing pancakes for us. He enjoyed cooking for the girls and me. He was a messy cook, though, leaving pans all over the counters.

Joseph lightly brushed the pancakes with butter at the table, and he served them to our daughters with strawberries after he dotted them with whipped topping.

Rabia yanked on the tablecloth to get her own plate. "Girls, be patient, Dad is working in a hurry," I scolded. Joseph fixed my spinach omelet while the girls devoured their treat. Soon Fatima and Rabia had whipped cream all over their pink shirts, and they giggled with their dad while I nibbled on my omelet, which was too crusty.

Joseph turned to me. "Estell, I know that you and the girls are going to have a good trip. I just want you to know that I will be sad without my family." I flashed my eyes at him and gave a faint smile.

At nine-thirty, I was rushing around the apartment looking for Rabia's pink boots. Fatima was playing in the closet with Buddy. "Girls, this is not playtime," I told them. "Fatima, I want you to wear this white jacket that Grandma Carrie gave you. Rabia, I found your boots, which were under the table." I got my tote bag, added chips and lollipops for the flight, and put it by the door with my two suitcases.

Before I left the apartment, I called their grandma, Carrie, so the girls could say goodbye again. After we hung up, Fatima asked, "When are we going to see Grammy?" I told her, "I'll talk to you about Grandma Carrie on the plane."

Joseph hailed us a cab. The four of us sat in the back seat, huddled together with small bags for the thirty-minute ride to La Guardia Airport. As we exited the vehicle, Rabia stared at the planes. Fatima asked, "Mommy, are we getting on the plane?" "Yes," I told her. "We are going to Aberdeen."

Joseph carried Rabia, and I held onto Fatima. When we entered the terminal, I was surprised to see how big it was inside. Soon, Joseph saw the Southwest sign, and I checked us in and get our boarding passes. Next, we hurried to our gate, passing long lines of people waiting to buy food, and the smell of fresh coffee and croissants made me wish we had time to linger. But the clock at the gate displayed 10:30 a.m., and we had just made it. A voice came over the loudspeaker announcing, "All aboard!"

Joseph, with teary eyes, leaned down and embraced his daughters. Fatima and Rabia began to cry, and I heard Joseph mumble, "You listen to your grandma, and I love you, my sweet daughters!"

"Daddy, please come with us!" Fatima begged.

"I have to stay in New York, and I'll call you tonight," Joseph explained. Then, he stood and squeezed me tightly and kissed me. "Estell, I am going to be lonely without you."

Suddenly, my eyes filled with tears, and Joseph kept holding my hands. This was the first time I had been away from Joseph since he went to Vietnam. I finally had to walk away from my husband with tears rolling down my cheeks. I pulled Fatima away from her dad and carried Rabia, with my tote bag on my shoulder. As we entered the jet bridge, we turned and waved goodbye. We boarded the plane with Fatima holding onto her yellow blanket and Rabia gripping her teddy bear.

Our seats were in the middle of the plane. My daughters were frightened by the noise of the engines. Rabia was whining, and the flight attendant came over to give her a toy. Soon the plane lifted into the air, and Rabia fell asleep in my arms; Fatima was buckled in her seat. Soon, the plane was flying through in the air, and the ride was comfortable.

After ninety minutes, we landed at the airport in Columbus, Mississippi, where it was warm and sunny. As we exited into the terminal, a white man wearing overalls and a straw hat greeted us at the door. "How y'all?" he asked us. *Definitely, I am back home,* I thought.

We walked to the baggage claim area, where I picked up our luggage from the turnstile. As I looked around with my daughters, I saw Tom and Mary waiting for us. They rushed to hug the girls and me. Mary picked up Rabia, and I held Fatima's hand.

We located Tom's white Ford Galaxy in the parking lot; Tom stowed the suitcases in the trunk, and we got in and put on our seatbelts. Tom drove onto Highway 69 to Aberdeen. Mary held Rabia in her arms and said she couldn't believe I was leaving New York.

"I thought it would cheaper," I told her. "And you know that I'm adventurous!"

After a forty-minute drive, Tom pulled into the driveway at Matubba Street. Fatima and Rabia were asking for cookies and milk. Mary told them with a smile, "I am your Aunt Mary, and I'm going to take care of you."

When I walked into the living room, there was Mary's son Christopher Holliday, who was seven years old. I screamed when I saw him. He had round cheeks and was tall like his dad. I wrapped my arms around him, and he announced in a strong voice, "My name is Chris."

"Fatima, Rabia," I called, "come here and hug your cousin."

As I said to my sister, "Mary, Chris is such a handsome fellow," Mary's older son, Gregory, marched into the living in his jeans and T-shirt. He rushed to give me a bear hug.

"So, Greg, do you take care of your little brother?" I teased.

"Aunt Sis, he tries to boss me around at his age, but I make sure that he cleans up his room.

Momma and Daddy joined us in the living room. I embraced Daddy, and Momma kissed me on the cheek. I think she had snuff in her lower lip.

Greg asked me how long I was going to be there.

"I am staying for three days," I told him. "Then, I am heading back to New York, and we are moving south."

"I know that you had to persuade Uncle Richard to leave New York," Greg said.

"Let's just say he saw my point of view" was my response.

I got the girls settled in the bedroom and changed their clothes. Soon, Momma yelled, "Your husband is on the phone." I was happy to hear his voice, and Fatima and Rabia talked eagerly to their dad. I chatted with my mom while they did, sharing my daughters' eating routines and braiding their hair.

Later, Daddy said, "Sis, I am happy that my grandchildren are here. Do you have enough money for your move?"

"We are on a tight budget," I admitted. Daddy took out his wallet from his overall pocket, just like he did when I was a little girl, and gave me one hundred dollars. I gripped his arm. *My dad is the best!* I thought. I choked up with emotion, and all I could say was, "Thank you, Daddy."

On Saturday, I said goodbye to my girls. They were crying and hanging onto my jacket. I caressed them for five minutes, and then I ran out the door because I felt like crying with them. I knew they would be fine with my momma, but my legs were weak. My mother held her grandchildren, and I knew that they were safe. Tom and

Mary were waiting for me in the car, and as I got in, I heard Rabia screaming, "Mommy!"

My sister sat in the back of the car to console me. After a bumpy ride, I was at the Columbus airport and thanking Mary and Tom for their help. I embraced them and turned to carry my suitcase into the airport. As I entered the terminal to return to New York, I heard Mary holler, "I'll take care of the girls." I turned and waved goodbye, knowing that the next time I would see all of them, our home would be in the South.

16

Leaving New York

URING OUR MONTHS of looking for an apartment in New York, we realized how expensive it would be to get a larger place for our growing family. I thought moving to the South would be cheaper. Fatima and Rabia could ride their bikes in the front yard, and I could grow my hydrangeas like my sister, Mary.

When I came to New York, I thought it was temporary, just to explore for the summer. *Maybe I will find a job for the summer,* I'd thought, *and return to Tuskegee University in Alabama in the fall to study to be a teacher.* But then I met Joseph, the man of my dreams, and I embarked on a new way of life. After six months in the city, I married this soldier. Later, we had two beautiful daughters. As I became a mother, I found inner strength and confidence inside me that I hadn't realized was there.

I believed in Joseph, and I trusted him because he has stood by my side despite my shortcomings. He reminded me of my Southern upbringing, and of my dad getting up at dawn and working at city hall until late in the evening. He never wavered in taking care of our family. Also, I had learned from my family in Aberdeen about loyalty, sacrifice, and sticking together. Indeed, I want to mirror their work ethic and their values.

I was conflicted about leaving my home and friends in New York. One Thursday evening about nine-thirty after my family was asleep, I tiptoed into the living room to use my Singer sewing machine, which my husband gave me for my birthday. I was making pink dresses for Rabia and Fatima with sashes in the back.

When I was ten years old, I learned to sew quilt pieces with my mother, sticking my finger with the needles until I figure out how to use a thimble. I'd been hooked on sewing ever since. It kept my mind occupied.

As I sewed, I thought about the trip we would soon be taking. I knew our lives would change in so many ways.

On the road to Atlanta, I will see cotton fields by the highway that will remind me of my days on the plantation. But I survived those days of picking cotton and poverty. I know that I am stronger now, and I am pleased about my courage and my family. In Atlanta, I thought, *I will see Confederate monuments in the middle of the city and signs in the window that read* White Patrons Only.

As my thoughts wandered, I considered some of the other changes that had happened to me since I'd moved from the South. *I expect to see white people who are less friendly than those in New York, who will look at me with suspicion, like they're wondering,* Why are *you* shopping here? *the same way that happened to me and my friend Jasmine while shopping for earrings at Gimbel's in New York.*

Just getting dressed in the morning for work was something I hadn't thought much about until I came to New York. When I first arrived, I just grabbed a dress from the closet each day without giving it much thought. Often, I just powdered my shiny forehead, and I was just learning to use an eyeliner to highlight my eyes.

Soon after I attended business school, I looked for a job. But since my only work experience had been as a maid in Aberdeen, I had no idea how to look put-together and wear conservative, professional attire. I first went to Express Employment Agency on Forty-Fifth Street and Seventh

Avenue to find a job. A woman who looked like my mother took me aside and told me, "Listen, Estell, you are a beautiful girl, but no one is going to hire you with those open-toe shoes and bright red lipstick." That was the best advice, and it helped me land my first job at Guerlain Perfume in a plush office on Fifth Avenue. Later, I learned to invest in my attire and my appearance and finally wear garments that told the world who I was.

Packing for Our Move

Our apartment was filled with stacks of taped boxes; we had been packing for the last five days. On that warm April afternoon, I wore my beige leisure pants and my pink quilted house shoes. The windows were open because it was stuffy in the apartment. I was getting tired from cleaning out the closets, and I yelled for Joseph.

"I am drinking my espresso coffee," he mumbled. Then he strolled into the living room. He looked around and gestured to the mess on the floor. "Why do you have all these clothes piled in the middle of the floor?"

"I am clearing out the clutter from the closets, and I decided to donate these clothes and toys to Goodwill," I told him.

"You got my blue Knicks jacket in the cardboard box … and with my cap!" Joseph said, rummaging through the box.

"Listen, Joseph," I said patiently, "the leather jacket is peeling on the collar, and your cap is fading. I know they have sentimental value, but I think it's time to let go."

Joseph continued surveying the room. "Estell, I don't see that old trunk you brought from Aberdeen with that rusty handle."

"All right, I'll throw that away," I said. "But I am taking *Homecoming,* my poems by Sonia Sanchez, and all of my books. I suppose you plan to keep all of your Miles Davis jazz albums."

"I am leaving most of those with my brother Herbie. By the way, he is coming over to help us pack.

I heard a knock on the door, and I opened it to greet our friends Jasmine and Noah. Noah held a brown shopping bag from the TJ Cajun restaurant on the corner. The smell of spicy chicken with Cajun rice reminded me how hungry I was from packing. Jasmine held out a smaller bag and said, "I know you told me no gifts, but I bought these small gold statues of the Empire State Building and the Statue of Liberty for your trip."

"Thank you," I told her. "This was the perfect gift to remind us of our friendship."

Joseph grabbed the plastic plates and announced, "Let's eat!" Then he said to Noah, "My wife and I needed a break from cleaning out the closets and taping boxes."

In the meantime, I chatted with Jasmine about the fun we had at Coney Island Beach with my daughters and her son, Erik. Jasmine said, "I enjoyed walking on the sand, dipping our feet into the water, and laughing as our strawberry Italian ices dripped through our fingers."

I thought about our weekends, remembering that we shopped on Fifth Avenue at Gimbel's for shoes on Saturdays, and then we ate pizza at Chelsea Café until our stomachs were about to pop.

In the living room, the guys packed the lamps and picture frames while listening to the Mets baseball game. Soon, Jasmine followed me into my daughter's room to wrap their teddy bears and dolls in bubble wrap. After two hours of packing, the large plastic tubs and boxes were lined up against the wall, and our friends were ready to leave.

We made our way to the front door, and with a smile, I thanked them for their help. Joseph and Noah shook hands and huddled together. Suddenly, Jasmine embraced me and mumbled, "You are my best friend, and who am I going to share my secrets and doubts with?" We stood there holding hands. I told her, "I will miss your smile," and Jasmine's voice cracked as she said, "I will never forget you, Estell." I could barely lift my arm to wave goodbye.

After they were gone, I checked my daughter's bedroom and saw green and yellow scribbled on the wall by Fatima's bed, And I saw more marks near the window, Rabia's red circles made with her crayons. *There are so many memories in my home.*

Many things in New York had become a part of our lives that strengthened our marriage and kept my family grounded in our moral values. I knew I would miss going to the mosque with the large silver dome on Riverside Drive with Joseph. There, I learned to expand my faith in God and my prayers in Arabic.

I recalled my daughters praying with me at the mosque; we wore pink floral-print dresses, and I wore my head scarf. For Jumu'ah (Friday worship service), Fatima and Rabia kneeled beside me and prayed, putting their foreheads on the prayer rug. When I looked over at them, I felt so much love for my young daughters. I wanted them to grow up and know their heritage. I taught them the Islamic greeting *"As-Salamu Alaykum,"* which means "Peace Be with You."

On our last day at the mosque, Iman Rashid gave my husband the name of a mosque in Atlanta, located in the West End neighborhood where we would attend worship. The Iman also offered financial assistance.

Joseph had made so many friends at the mosque, and I had never seen him so happy. He found men there who believed in his cause for social justice and supported him. I knew that he felt a sense of peace and hope with his friends and would miss them.

Ready for Atlanta

On Thursday morning, I woke up at 7:00 a.m. The apartment was empty except for a loveseat and a couple of chairs. Our four suitcases were packed. I thought back to when I found this apartment before Joseph came home from Vietnam. I was so excited to rent an apartment on my own and to decorate my living room with my red loveseat and matching curtains. The place made me feel special.

Moreover, I could hear Fatima's laughing in her pink bedroom while she played with Buddy. And I could see Rabia making her first steps in her white sandals at twelve months old. I could hear Joseph playing his boombox to the toe-tapping sounds of Motown with Diana Ross's "Ain't No Mountain High Enough."

I had done a walkthrough the previous day with the landlady and handed her the keys. She was a kind person, but I was truly going to miss my home.

On Friday at 9:00 a.m., I gazed at our home, the brownstone on the second floor at 621 Halsey Street, for the last time. *I have so many stories to tell my children and grandchildren. Wow, I experienced so much happiness here, and this feeling will now continue in Atlanta.*

Our two-story brownstone was located on 621 Hancock Street in Brooklyn, New York. I decided to live here because it was the center of African American culture. It was surrounded by Caribbean and Southern restaurants, and there was a Jewish deli about two blocks away. Photo credit: iStock.com/Auseklis

Home was where I could kick off my shoes; I could cry; I could laugh. I could get on my knees when times got rough and talk to God about my dreams for my family. I remember when my daughters were born, I felt so happy when I saw their faces. I was thrilled to be a mom. Joseph and I celebrated like we had won the lottery. By this time, Joseph was putting our luggage in the maroon Chevrolet. I packed a small box and a cooler with our roast beef sandwiches on wheat bread, four apples, and chips. This reminded me of my momma fixing a greasy cardboard box with hot wings and potato salad for me when I came to New York on the Trailways bus. That trip, I had ninety-eight dollars in my pocket, and I rode the bus for two days. Now, I was returning to the South with big dreams and with my husband and my two daughters. I felt grateful for my family and the lessons that I learned about being a woman.

I am connected to the South because of my parents and my spiritual upbringing, I thought. But growing up in Aberdeen had been bittersweet. I'd left the South to escape the economic conditions and inequality in education. Back then, I was called a Negro and excluded because of my gender and race.

Frankly, Aberdeen wasn't big enough for me, and I sought an opportunity to grow. New York City was just the place with its bright lights, the subway, tall skyscrapers, and hordes of people who looked like me.

I am returning to the South for a fresh start and to improve our lives economically. I want a house with space, something bigger than a closet, where my family can live comfortably and be happy. I want to look out a window and see leaves falling to the ground and crabgrass growing in the backyard.

I realized that Joseph and I made a decision that was going to change our lives. Not knowing what to expect, we concluded that we would make our own path. I saw possibilities for us to live a better life. When I was younger, I just thought about my needs. *As a woman with a husband and two daughters, I have a new perspective on life. My family comes first!*

Joseph drove past Jefferson Avenue, where I met him in 1964 with my cousin Elizabeth. He cruised past Thompkins Avenue where I shopped for my first dashiki from a small storefront.

Joseph turned the dial on the radio to WWRL radio, and I nodded to the sound of "Lean on Me" by Bill Withers. I rolled down the window, and the damp morning air flashed across my face. I planned on sleeping for much of this long ride, so I was wearing my yellow head scarf, my black T-shirt with a bold logo that read "Just a Girl from Brooklyn," and my bell-bottom jeans and sandals. I also brought along several bed pillows to relax my back. I cast a glance at Joseph, who wore a plaid shirt, casual pants, and black sunglasses.

Joseph steered the car while occasionally glancing at the road map to Georgia. He looked at me with a grin. I smiled back and thought, *I am enjoying this trip with my husband because our souls are connected, and I have embraced our past. As poet and writer Maya Angelou wrote, "My mission in life is not merely to survive, but to thrive." Now, it is time for a new direction for my family.*

"Guess what," Joseph announced, "I am driving you through Harlem." This was just what I needed to reminisce. He passed the Apollo Theatre with its iconic marque on 125th Street near Seventh Avenue, where we saw Aretha Franklin. I smiled as I thought about how we went to Sylvia's Restaurant for chicken and waffles after the concert.

Soon, Joseph was driving by the brownstone with a big green fern on the stoop. "That's where we got married seven years ago, just three days before you left for Vietnam," I reminisced. "You were wearing your green army uniform from Fort Bragg, North Carolina, and you were clean-shaven."

"Estell, you wore those tall, black suede boots with the stacked heels."

"I wasn't used to wearing heels, and my legs were wobbling," I said, laughing.

Joseph kept teasing me. "When you came from Aberdeen, you wore that pink striped dress that was too big for you and those wide, red hoop earrings." "Shut up!" I told him, but next he said, "When I looked at you now, I see my queen and the mother of my children."

"You are such a charmer," I said as I ruffled his hair. "I know that you were a little crazy asking me to get married after two months. Then you became a rebel and joined the Panther Party. But I fell for your charm."

I glanced at the speedometer. "Hey Joseph, I think you should stick to the speed limit," and he responded that he was being mindful of the thirty-five-miles-per-hour signs.

Joseph was quiet for a moment, and then he said, "Estell, I really miss our daughters."

I told him, "I talked to them this morning. Fatima said, 'Mommy, when are you and dad coming for us?' And Rabia asked about Buddy. I did my best to cheer them up. Gosh, I want to see their little faces." Thinking about our daughters made us both smile.

Shortly after, we were in the Bronx near Amsterdam Avenue, and Joseph looked for a parking place at the curb. I exited the car that was filled with pillows and toys. Joseph grabbed the red roses that he had purchased for his mother with a tag saying, "I am so proud to be your son."

Carrie opened the door, and the smell of coffee brewing on the stove greeted us. Once we were settled inside, Buddy jumped up on Joseph with a bark of happiness, and I rubbed his brown-and-white fur.

"Come sit on the brown couch," said Carrie. "Joseph, I knew you and Estell were coming, so I brewed Maxwell House coffee for you; Estell, I fixed your peppermint tea."

As we sat on the sofa, Buddy crawled up and laid his head on my lap. I opened my purse and fed Buddy his small crunchy Meaty Bones.

Surprised by the unexpected treat, he ate the whole bag. I glided my hand across his back, and he wagged his tail.

Joseph talked to his mom about our trip to Atlanta and thanked her for keeping our Buddy forever. I wasn't really listening; instead, I gazed at the yellow bean bags where my daughters watched television and nibbled on sugar cookies.

I reminded Carrie about the Saturday afternoon when she taught me how to make chicken cacciatore and told me that Joseph liked it spicy with heavy sauce. I prepared this meal for my husband's dinner, and he devoured it. Carrie added, "You did burn up a few pots in the beginning. However, you are a fine cook now!"

Finally, Joseph said, "Mother, we are leaving."

Carrie turned to me and said, "Estell, I want you to have this gift."

I opened the silver box and found a pearl strand necklace, which she told me had been in the family for years. I thanked her, and with a warm hug, I said, "I will cherish these pearls.

"Estell, you brought so much joy into my life when you married my son and had my two grandchildren. Oh my God, I going to miss my family!" She put her head on my shoulder and began to weep. I wrapped my arms around her tightly, and I felt her thick gray hair on my shoulder for the last time.

Joseph embraced his mother and kissed her on the forehead. I saw his eyes tear up as he held her long, wrinkled fingers. She said, "Joseph, remember that you are driving in the South and with Estell.

"I know, Mommy," he said. "I'll call you when we get to Atlanta."

My legs were weak as I waved to Carrie, and Joseph dragged his feet. I grabbed his hand as we headed to our car. For a few minutes, I leaned into him beside the car because at that moment, I just wanted to cry. Separating from Carrie and my friends was so painful.

Joseph said, "Estell, no matter what happens, I will always be by your side." I removed my sunglasses, and my husband squeezed my hand as a few tears rolled down my cheeks.

"Joseph, I am scared, but I am ready to make this journey with you. You mean so much to me, and you are my inspiration." We eased into the car and put on our seat belts.

After we pulled away from the curb, Joseph told me he was stopping at the bodega (corner grocery store) to get Coca-Colas, and he asked if I wanted a bag of Doritos. I told him I did, and a Twix candy bar.

As he drove, I told my husband, "It's tough to leave Brooklyn, and after living here for ten years, I love this place. I wish Fatima and Rabia were here in the back seat so I could touch their cheeks and hear them say, 'Mommy!' I am lonely without my daughters."

"We are following our dreams," Joseph replied.

The car felt empty, even with all the junk around us, and chills came over me. I prayed for God to help us on our journey. Joseph stopped for gas at the Shell station to fill up the tank at $1.39 a gallon. I just sat in the car, quietly pondering about Atlanta.

Joseph, strapped on his seat belt, ignited the engine. Finally, we headed to West 179th Street and Cabrini, the entrance to the George Washington Bridge, which is a double-decker suspension bridge that spans the Hudson River. Surrounded by misty morning fog, the bridge was a beautiful sight.

"Joseph, can you believe that we're getting onto the bridge? I am leaving Manhattan, my home," I said with a sigh. As the traffic crawled along and I watched the city's skyscrapers fade in the background, I imagined the flashing lights of Broadway, and I could still smell the pungent and musty air from the subway.

"I am going to re-create my identity with new people and start fresh, create a better life. I am building a new path." I balled up my pink handkerchief in my hands because I was both excited about moving to Atlanta and sad about leaving Manhattan. Joseph looked at me. I took off my sunglasses; they were hiding my watery eyes.

I am from the plantation, and Joseph is from the streets of Harlem. We have a strong bond that just happened. Now, we are headed to a new life.

Joseph squeezed my hand and said gently, "We will make this work."

After we'd been driving for a while, my husband asked, "Are you ready to see those blooming dogwood trees in Atlanta?"

Indeed, I was ready! We were headed to Atlanta, often referred to as "Hotlanta," with its Southern hospitality and warm weather. I could imagine sitting on the back porch and chomping on a slice of watermelon in the summer with mosquitoes humming around me. I supposed that could be fun. But all I said to my husband was, "I am ready for our new home."

It started to drizzle, and I listened to the windshield wipers scrape across the glass. "I feel like we are climbing a mountain together," I told Joseph. "I am uprooting my life, and I am starting over with mixed feelings. The hardest part of leaving New York is learning to let go of our past to pursue our new dreams."

This move to Atlanta was a new beginning for my family; as the miles went by, I couldn't help but wonder what life would be like in the future for Joseph and me.

c❧⃝

My journey began in Aberdeen, Mississippi. I came to New York on a Trailway bus with my suitcase and $98.00. I was scared, and I prayed a lot. It was my Southern upbringing that guided me forward. The stability that I learned from my parents gave me an understanding of what a family should look like. It was the love in that little white house on Matubba Street that made me smile.

I started my family with Joseph, a Vietnam veteran, and our two daughters. Joseph brought with him our culture and showered our daughters with love. Joseph was faithful and hardheaded at times, but he was strong like my dad. I continued my faith in God, worked hard, and persevered through segregation.

From a maid in Aberdeen to a professional model in New York, I made choices that changed my life. I pushed through and held my head up like my momma always told me. I finally learned to speak up as a Black woman and carry on the struggle for equal justice with my husband. I shared with my girls' a pride in their history, and they are beautiful new blossoms on my family tree. From New York to Atlanta, I now carry the legacy of the Sims family and uphold the importance of having a strong family structure for the Halliburtons.

Thank you for reading *Leaving Aberdeen: Memoir of a Southern Girl*. I hope you've enjoyed reading my story as much as I've enjoyed sharing it with you. Please consider leaving a short review wherever you purchased this book to help other readers decide if they might enjoy it too.

I'd love to hear from you and connect on social media, too. Please visit me:

Facebook: https://www.facebook.com/estell.sims/
Instagram: https://www.instagram.com/estell.s/
LinkedIn: https://www.linkedin.com/in/estell-halliburton-78100349/
TikTok: https://www.tiktok.com/@brownsugar1945?

The story of the Halliburtons doesn't end here. When Joseph, Fatima, Rabia, and I left New York, we had no idea what adventures waited for us.

Please visit my website at http://www.leavingaberdeen.com for updates about the next book in this series.

Acknowledgments

I want to thank my professors at Georgia State University-Perimeter College in Dunwoody, Georgia, for introducing me to biology, history, and psychology. These classes initiated a new vision of the world and expanded my curiosity.

At the GSU library, I met Reference Specialist Dr. Mary Etta Thomas, who was kind and knowledgeable. She helped me evaluate information through the databases to see what I needed for my class project. And when I told her I was writing my memoir, she encouraged me and offered her support.

When I was going to the Writing Lab for help with my English essays, I met Gelia Dolcimascolo, a friendly lady who listened to my short stories and invited me to join the Writers' Circle with other authors. I read my short narrative and received constructive feedback. Gelia is an author, writer/poet, and writing tutor at GSU's Perimeter College, and through her support, I gained new ideas and confidence.

I joined TRiO Student Support Services on campus at GSU-Perimeter to increase my academic success. I met two educational specialists, Tracye Paggett and Larry Thomas, Jr. Not only did I find good counseling, but I met two caring advisors. Tracye motivated me to keep going when I was struggling in my math class, and I did well in the class. Thank you for your support, TRiO!

A special note of appreciation goes to my siblings: my brothers, Alfred and Wardell Sims, Jr, and my sister, Mary Holliday. I want to thank them for fun times and treating me special as a little sister.

To my daughters: Fatima Sparks, Rabia Nelsons, and Aisha Halliburton I want to thank you for believing in my vision to write my story and helping me get my book published. Of course, I was happy when they brought a strawberry shake from Chick-fil-A … thank you, my cheerleaders!

To my grandchildren: Xavier Sparks, Selena Sparks, Khadijah Muhammad, Amina Kadric, Azra Kadric, and Aaliyah Kadric. They came over to hang out with me at Morgan Falls Park on Saturday mornings and eat my freshly baked chocolate chip cookies. I want to thank them for filling my life with so many hugs.

To my nephews: Gregory Sims, Wardell Sims, and my cousin Billy Sims. I want to thank you for sharing many family stories with me and continuing our legacy.

To my New York family: Anthony Halliburton, Leishea Halliburton, Michael Wilson, Sharyme Wilson. Thank you for all the great memories, and I treasure your love.

I want to thank my editor, Candace Johnson. Just a few months ago, we were strangers. I was somewhat skeptical because I saw a picture of a woman with white skin and blonde hair from the Pacific Northwest. I was not sure that she could understand or empathize with my experiences of growing up as a Black girl in Mississippi. I emailed her the twenty-five pages of my memoir, which eventually became the pages of this book. Through this journey, Candace provided me the space to express my feelings and my story, which I greatly appreciate. I would recommend Candace as an editor with good insight.

Finally, I want to thank the many relatives and friends who reached out to me on social media, telephone calls, and sent me flowers. I am grateful for your support.

About the Author

Estell Sims Halliburton's love for her family has always been her foundation—first the sharecropping family she was born into on a plantation in rural Mississippi, and later the family she created with her husband, Joseph. Her first memoir, *Leaving Aberdeen: A Memoir of a Southern Girl,* is the story of her early years set against the backdrop of systemic racism, the turbulent social upheaval of the 1960s, and her journey to find her voice and her place in the world as a Black woman, the wife of a Black Panther, and a young mother who dreamed of a better life for her daughters.

Estell attended Tuskegee University for one year before moving to New York City, where she met Joseph R. Halliburton, a US Army soldier on his way to Vietnam. After a whirlwind romance, the couple married, and Estell worked in accounting and as a fashion model while her husband fought overseas.

Her dream of having a family of her own soon came true, and the birth of two of her three daughters highlighted for her the importance of advocating for her views and adding her voice to a generation that came of age during the social turbulence of the 1960s and '70s. Later, Estell was blessed to be a stay-at-home mom for many years. After her daughters were grown and her beloved husband passed away, she returned to college, where she discovered her love for storytelling. Majoring in education, Estell graduated from Georgia State University-Dunwoody in 2021.

Today, Estell lives in Atlanta, Georgia. She is a mother of three, a grandmother of six grandchildren, and a great-grandmother of two. She gets up at 5:30 every morning to drink her green tea and do her yoga exercises before she begins writing. Some days will find her getting her nails painted red, and shopping at Perimeter Mall for a new fancy purse. Other times, she is baking moist banana bread with her daughters to share with the grandchildren. One of her daughters and a granddaughter live with her and their Siamese cat, Snow, who likes to sit on the windowsill. Learn more about Estell and her plans for writing more about her family at http://www.leavingaberdeen.com.

CPSIA information can be obtained
at www.ICGtesting.com
Printed in the USA
FSHW010706180122
87713FS